W9-COU-610

Mothering Through Pain and Suffering in Silence

A collection of Stories

From

SURVIVORS

Cover Design Graphics by Kenneth Caldwell
Back cover photography Legacy X

Table of Contents

Mothering Through the Pain

Endorsements

"Jasmine Boudah takes readers on a healing journey of Black mothers. This book delivers unspoken truths and inspiration for Black women who have bared children or who face traumatic obstacles in life. It is full of constructive and revealing stories of several Black women. This book is for both women and men who want to understand the experience Black mothers endure from conception. Black mothers must heal from the pain of the past and produce a legacy of healing. Our children deserve parents at their superior health. This book provides awareness for us all to provide a better future for our children."

-Brandon Jones, Psychotherapist

"Mothering through Pain and Suffering in Silence: A collection of Stories from Survivors is a much needed beginning to the discussion and healing of Black Motherhood and Mothers. For centuries we've been taught to hide our pain or even worse that it is what makes us who we are as women, loves…
mothers. Yet Jasmine offers us refuge in her words and her allowing space for others to share. Our strength as this book points out is our ability to love and nurture through it all. Our silence speaks volumes and as we share our truths and listen to the stories of others we uplift, enlighten and advance ourselves and each other. Jasmines brave exploration is a refreshingly vulnerable and

triumphant account of Motherhood for women of Afrikan descent. Allow your heart to be refreshed as you read this book."

-Milele
Author of "Confessions of a Sage Woman"(2016), "Confessions of a faithful woman" (2012) and upcoming "Sage Wisdoms" and "Conversations with my sons" (2017)

"Ideally, the restoration of a people lies in the health of the woman. Mothering Through Pain and Suffering in Silence is a vital echo of experiences that begins or continues the dialogue of restoring the "wombman", the progenitor of Black heritage, survival, and greatness. The authors provide visceral, timeless accounts of pain to strength moments that become the hallmark of Black women's social existence. Further, the pages do more than just reposition our hearts and souls, it provokes and inspires the framework to envision the Black "wombman's" life without pain. This reading is necessary for any Black man's journey to truly comprehend and experience the indispensable level of love, compassion, and daily healing and protection of 'her' soul, heart, mind, and body. The words from this book are not only healing for her, but remedial for a Black man's definition of himself."

-Adrian Mack, Black Family Educator

Foreword

We live in a time of perfectly curated feeds. Filters on our cameras have become filters for our lives and motherhood is no exception. We are seemingly always happy. Our children are seemingly always cute. Birthday parties are seemingly always joyful. Let the world tell it, *and truly let us tell it*, through the lens of blogs and social media particularly, we are more than strong. We are downright superhuman. The problem with this process of self-curation is that it masks our pain, lends itself to comparison, and often leads to isolation. *It is the antithesis of healing, sisterhood, and community.*

Enter "Mothering Through Pain and Suffering In Silence: A Collection of Stories from Survivors."

There are some works in life born out of desire; others that fill a void and give voice to silence. This is such a work. The project provides the backdrop for Black wombmen to have a new conversation in this space of self-curation.

Raw and vulnerable this collection tables unspoken realities within our collective walk and ushers us from the all too common "likes" and "she's so cute" into an intimate space of "I see you goddess," "you are not alone," and "me too."

Not a series about the negative experiences of Black mothers but, ultimately of their triumph and covering topics from rape to abortion to abuse, miscarriages, postpartum depression and more, each submission is as unique as its author; told in its own voice, *without a filter*. Each story provides the reader with a unique opportunity to understand, relate, empathize, admire, and yes, to celebrate. It is tales of Black wombmen's relentless ability to love, forgive, and connect spiritually to this thing called motherhood.

If there is one thing my work with women along with my own experiences has taught me, is the fact that few things in life are as powerful as sisterhood and the feeling of being seen and understood. No other group of women in this country has had to mother and render children through such extreme adversity like the Black wombman. Given this context, each story is a testament to divine nature of Black mothers.

As a mother, I was honored to share my story. As a reader, I was deeply connected to the words of these queens, most strangers, now sisters; to their voices. They are a tribute to the millions of women, living and transitioned, with shared, untold stories. I will that as you read each page, you see yourself reflected and celebrated even in those experiences which may not share and that you are encouraged to have less filtered, more honest conversations about the beautiful, complex walk of Black motherhood. May your find your voice in this process and the courage use it for good.

Nikolai Pizarro Author of Ring the Alarm: A Zero to Five Parenting Guide for Low-Income Black and Latino Caregivers

Introduction

In the pages that follow, you will be immersed in the lives of several astonishing Black women who are the descendants of enslaved Africans in the Americas. These women share heart wrenching stories of how they have grappled vigorously with the unforgiving circumstances they are confronted with as mothering is juxtaposed with their Black bodies while living in America. Seen in this way, living in this peculiar nation, given the inherently flawed foundation that has been paved by systemic racism, has created a vicious cycle of destruction for the Black woman, and many fail to talk about it in great detail. In this book, the contributing authors will be referred to as *Black wombmen* to give honor to the divine position we hold on this planet being the first Mothers of Civilization whose wombs bring forth life alongside the Creator. The wombman possess a power so divine that many attempts have been made to separate us from the power of our wombs. It a spiritual connection between the Black wombman's yoni (vagina), womb (the portal of life), her heart, her soul and her mind. This attempt to strip of this power is reflected in the state of our communities and relationships. Understanding the divine essence of the Black wombman is extremely important for the sustainability of our future generations.

All of these contributing wombmen have voiced and delved deeply into their life experiences as Black wombmen combatting what has been coined and continually normalized and reinforced as the "Black superwoman" or "strong Black woman" archetypes.

These archetypes paint vivid pictures of us miraculously rising above the fray and appearing to remain in one piece regardless of the many devastating blows society and sometimes our own community heaves our way. The message is loud and clear, "If we don't get shit done, who will?"

Unfortunately, what is often devoid from the conversation, because it has been deemed taboo to talk about, is what is under the surface of the Black wombmen's experience living here in America. The trauma we endure throughout the process, because after all we are strong Black women who stoically carry the weight of the world on our shoulders without skipping a beat, IS THE SAME TRAUMA we have CARRIED for decades in this country. This trauma can no longer be ignored by writing it off as simply what strong Black women are made to endure. Our capacity to love and function as we take care of our families and community should not be measured by how much pain we can endure silently. The wombmen whose voices and stories grace the pages that follow come from many different walks of life, but share the experience of carrying trauma and doing so in pain and silence as a direct result of our trepidations and history in this nation. We call for the support of our village in the name of revolution for our children, families and community.

In many ways, we are astronomically strong and extremely capable of getting things done and enduring difficult times, because we have always had to do so. Conversely, the existence of these archetypes abound with assumptions and are coupled with the deadly ramifications that institutionalized racism has placed on our community. This strips us of our right to choose our role in society in many spaces because the choice has been made before many of us exited our mother's womb.

The reality is we must march on boldly and indestructibly because our lives, the lives of our children, and the lives of our legacies depend on us making a way even when there appears to be no way. Furthermore, there is practically a slither of space to be our authentic selves in many spaces as a direct result of our circumstances and experiences as Black wombmen in this country, particularly Black wombmen who are mothering. While we take pride in our role as mother we wear the mask well and neglect our emotions out of the harsh reality that we simply do not have the privilege of taking time for ourselves to indulge in too much self-care and feeling.

The time has come for Black wombmen to have a space to share many of their truths. Truths they haven't uttered to even their closest friends for fear of the desensitization or cognizant dissonance engulfed responses we are often met with when attempting to disclose our truths and realities to others. When we attempt to share our authentic experiences we are met with "but girl, you are a strong Black woman, you will be okay." This response is a form of abuse and the cycle must stop one wombman, one child, one family, and one community at a time. Brother Malcolm X once said, "The most disrespected person in America is the Black woman. The most unprotected person in America is the Black woman. The most neglected person in America is the Black woman." In light of this, it is my hope that co-creating a platform for these wombmen, including myself, to unapologetically share our naked truths with the world, but more importantly with our own communities, will encourage a critical dialogue around the paradigm shift that needs to take place. This collection of stories is an intervention geared towards healing, uplifting and supporting the restorative care of our Black wombmen, which in turn will provide more opportunities for us to live authentically and have our humanity restored in a revolutionary way. Living authentically and having our humanity restored will spark a change in the way we are conditioned to interact with life, the world, our communities, even our children and our life partners. Disclosing the challenges faced daily and the burdens we bear will better position us to continue to mother in ways widely inaccessible to many of us for a vast majority of our lives. Sharing our stories will set us free and create spaces to heal and be restored without restrictions and the choke holds of the strong Black superwoman complex violating our humanity. We are humans worthy of humanity and although we are "superwomen," it should be a viable option to take off our capes if and when we so choose.

While this is a collection of stories from Black wombmen I have personally encountered over the duration of my lifetime, (although only 28 years), I do not proclaim that this collection of stories can speak to the vast experiences of every single Black wombman in America. However, many of the themes presented are amplified in the lives of many of the wombmen I know and have encountered in my life. I realize that my sisters of the diaspora and their unique struggles are not necessarily represented in this collection and I acknowledge that we stand in solidarity with them as well.

African Black wombman born in America experience a unique set of struggles as a direct result of the harsh conditions of slavery that sought to strip us from our culture, strip our men of their power and invoke a trauma that would linger in our DNA for generations to come. Slavery gave birth to the strong Black superwoman and the creation is still damaging us today. Much of what we experienced during slavery is haunting us today. Knowing this as I've moved through life, I am hyper vigilant about the fact that the theme of mothering through pain and suffering in silence has remained a poignant pillar in the journeys of many of my Black wombmen, sistah-friends and goddesses who have bore children or who are mothering to some capacity.

These challenges we face must be discussed in order to move toward community building and establishing a strong presence of Black revolutionary love. Black wombmen are the ultimate heroines; but we cannot do it alone. We invite you to take this walk with us and birth new narratives by loving on every Black wombman you encounter from this day forward.

Jasmine Tane't Boudah

An Open Letter to the Black Lotus Mothers:

My Dearest Black Lotus Mother(s),

We live in a nation where our divine goddess potential has been hidden from us in the most damaging ways. Sadly, with countless instances of neglect and being met with the classic phrase "but you're a strong Black woman you can handle anything", your wall got a little higher to shield yourself and your stoic demeanor thickened because feeling was a privilege not afforded to a Black wombman who was more than capable of endearing the weight of the world. But like roses that have grown from concrete, and phoenixes that have risen from the ashes, you have survived. By digging deeply into your limitless soul you have managed again to sacrifice yourself for the advancement of our community by sharing your stories that are wrought with transparency, power and healing. For that my thank you is a thousand-fold because I have no doubt in my mind that we will spark a revolution as we move forward and allow our pain to birth our purpose.

I never could have imagined that my own story would touch so many of you and provide a space and a platform to talk about what happened to us behind closed doors. My promise to each of you is that I will carry your stories with me throughout my life as I continue to mother through my own pain. You have shared parts of your tattered hearts and for that I will be forever grateful because I too am changed.

You are the epitome of strong Black women because you have chosen to challenge the archetype. After all you have been through you are abounding daily attempts to break the vicious cycle and pour into precious royalty, your children. It is no easy feat to pour lovingly into your children when you are experiencing this pain with very little relief, but you are not victims--- you are survivors, and being the composer of your own narrative shifts the power. I pray that you master the peace within as you as every broken piece is healed. May your very being become saturated with golden flakes of supreme divineness as you blossom into the lotus flower that you are.

Know that I think of each of you and your inimitable stories and give honor to you. I think of every time you were convinced it was acceptable to be vulnerable and someone took advantage of your vulnerability and missed an opportunity to truly uplift and support you. I think of every time you cried out for a shoulder to lean on and a helping hand to embrace you to lessen the pain inflicted by your fall. Although you are warriors you should not have to prepare for battle daily and carry your armor alone.

As supreme Goddesses and mothers of this civilization you all are worthy of that unconditional love that makes space for you to take off your cape and express your moment of weakness. My wish for you all is that your lives be like poetic waterfalls etched into the cerebellum of each soul whose eyes grace each page of your stories. There is no turning back once you have recognized your infinite power to challenge the status quo and leap bounds in writing your own narratives. I am more compassionate about understanding each of you because you are my Sister Queens and because our souls speak the same language. Our souls speak of the agony of carrying so many stories and tears untold. Bravely and furiously facing our hard trials is necessary to establish truth within our community and us. You all are a magnificent balance between abundance and sacristy.

May you be free to experience the world in a more humanistic light. May you be surrounded and protected by the Almighty Creator, your ancestors and a mighty village of genuinely compassionate supporters as you continue to use your magic to make the world spin. May you continue to love until infinity goes beyond the limitations that have been set on the love a Black woman is capable of giving!

Let your melanin shine bright and spark a fire in every soul you encounter because you are the true testament of what love is and can be regardless of the box society attempts to put you in daily. Let us all draw near with a true heart and in abundant assurance and faith that we deserve to have the opportunity to be vulnerable and human. Through our stories we are shaking up the world and fighting for our sisters who need to take their royal places in this world as goddesses and mothers of the universe.

In love, abundance and solidarity,

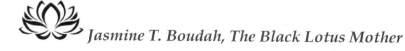 *Jasmine T. Boudah, The Black Lotus Mother*

With permission of composer, A.C Lewis, I'd like to dedicate this first poem to all of the Black "wombmen" I've encountered, and to those I've not had the privilege of meeting and building with yet. I carry you in my heart daily because you are my sisters in this revolution. Black wombmen are goddesses who continue to bear the cross of this nation day in and day out. My eternal wish is that someone in this world is able to see your soul fully and abundantly and allow you to be human in the midst of your responsibilities, your struggles, your pain, your hardships as well as all of your joys. After all, super-wombmen deserve to take off their capes from time to time and be restored, uplifted and healed because we cannot pour from empty cups.

Open My Soul

(Chorus)
If you could peel back my eyelids to open my soul

What would you see, what would you see?
If you could peel back my eyelids to open my soul

What would you see, what would you see?
If you could peel back my eyelids to open my soul

What would you see, what would you see?
If you could peel back my eyelids to open my soul

What would you see, what would you see?

My memories, that I'm deteriorating spiritually,
The few [wo]men whose lifestyles I'm mirroring
Peering deeper

It would appear that I'm veering off the road that's
paved for me.
Foot on the gas with no steering for faithlessly, I roam
Hence my senseless ambition
All alone, would need a clone to relate to my position
So few of us, I'm blessed by only thinking about the
troubles
All they see is my success, I remember the struggles
Never comfortable, isolated, tiny little bubble
[Ms]. Oh-so-perfect building statues out of rubble
Making triumph out of trouble, everybody loves you
[Ms]. Headed-for-the-stars, often feels that she will
stumble
Now deep in my soul there is a key
Which unlocks all of the inner desires special to me
But the reason the aimlessly goal chasing

Is that I don't know myself well enough to locate it
My whole cadence is off, my soul beats
To the rhythm of my heart but my senses are so weak
What do I hear? What do I see?
What do I hear? What do I see?
I see confusion, somebody I'm abusing
A soul with many bruises, abrasions and contusions
Illusion's that I'm okay, through the bandages it's oozing
Hurt, pain and pride convoluted
I do this for everybody that feels misunderstood
For brothers [and sisters] stuck in college while their
hearts are in the hood
For those who walk that path until their toes hurt
And for those who know their worth but are still soul
searching

(Chorus)
If you could peel back my eyelids to open my soul

What would you see, what would you see?
If you could peel back her eyelids to open her soul

What would you see, what would you see?
If I could peel back her eyelids to open her soul

What would I see, what would I see?
If we could peel back her eyelids to open her soul

What would we see, what would we see?
Fifth customer tonight, since Rasheed's in the pen'
Gotta find a way to hustle, gotta feed these kids
That what she tells herself every night, by now she don't
feel it
The penetration of latex keeps these bills from building
She just stares at the ceiling, tabulating expenses
And he stares into her eyes, he mistakes it as pensive

Will she ever tell her man to whom she's vowed to be
loyal
The same action that saved her kids will more than
likely destroy him
And so she holds it in, until her heart is imploded in
Rotted and eroding, and she cannot keep control of it,
Her soul has been exploding since first exploiting her
passion
Although the first cut's deepest, our scars are made
from gashes
Philosophies start clashing when tested with extremes
Just a glimpse into her soul would show exactly what I
mean
The story of so many, lives treated like a myth
Just a glimpse into her soul would let you know that she
exists

(Chorus)
If you could peel back my eyelids to open my soul

What would you see, what would you see?
If you could peel back my eyelids to open my soul

What would you see, what would you see?
If they could peel back our eyelids to open our souls

What would they see, what would they see?
If they could peel back our eyelids to open our souls

What would they see, what would they see?

 *A. C. Lewis*

I AM STRONG

I am strong because after being abused while pregnant, the doctor said I was going to miscarry (my abuser sitting next to me). That night, I held my stomach and spoke to her, "If we are going to do this together, I need you to stop..."

Instantly, I bled no more.

I am strong because while pregnant I learned to protect my child even from myself; and that meant acknowledging the pain that dwells within me that tolerates pain from others, seeking help, and finally escaping the relationship.

I am strong because I moved back under my parents' roof; because providing my child with a stable environment surrounded with a loving village took precedence over my "own space."

I am strong because I delivered my child all natural, with no epidural, and no birthing classes (I couldn't afford them). So I learned to call upon the powers of all my ancestors; the mothers and women before me and around me. I trusted my body. I trusted her.

I am strong because I sought custody of my daughter; fighting past the anxiety and fear to ensure the safety and well-being of myself and of my child.

I am strong because I receive no form of support nor physical presence from her father yet. I choose to not project any feelings of abandonment, insecurity nor discontent but only of peace, security and happiness; I choose to be the filter. Because we are okay, we are supported and we are loved.

I am strong because I've chosen not to be sexually intimate since the conception of my daughter to strengthen my faith, clear my life of distraction, pursue growth, so I can hear God's voice clearer; to order my steps.

I am strong because living in a world in which superficial and artificial is the norm, I embrace and seek all that is natural and truth.

I am strong because I endured an extremely abusive relationship yet continued to demonstrate grace under pressure.

I am strong because despite my trials and not having my ideal circumstances, I wake up smiling ready to seize the day. Not just for Shannon, not to portray my life is perfect, but because I choose to focus on my blessings and show others they can do the same.

I am strong because I am a survivor.

I am strong because I am a mother.

And if nothing else, I AM STRONG and I AM BEAUTIFUL simply because I Am Human!

Ashley Wright, Creator of Ms. Wright's Way

That Mom!

I knew before we conceived our first child that I would breastfeed. I knew that it would be one of the greatest sacrifices that I could make as a mother, almost as important as our decision to have children. Being "that mom" was what I wanted and prayed to be....

So dear sons, I aspired to be *that mom* from the beginning and even today..... *that mom* who would consume only the healthiest food because I knew the life I had growing in me deserved nothing but the best from the beginning. I aspired to be *that mom* who became conscious of everything in my life that might impede your growth, development, and ultimate potential in life. I became *that mom* who read countless books, journal articles and asked every question on my list at each doctor's visit and chronicled every moment of each pregnancy.

I became *that mom* who relished in the thought of being a vessel for God's gift to your dad and me to receive nourishment through my body. How amazing, how wondrous it was to look into your eager eyes as you anticipated being fed from my bosom! How privileged did I feel to be able to provide comfort in a matter of seconds when your little world became overwhelming. It was not easy by any means, but I was determined from the beginning to be successful. So, in those days it took us to sync up I chose not to become frustrated but to stay the course until we figured out how to latch on properly, which hold seemed to work the best, how to avoid pulling off my nipple when it was time to switch breasts and how to rest easy knowing you were getting enough. The bond we formed could hardly be described by words. We were so in sync, and the love God blessed me with only grew stronger each day. So much so that my sacrifice would expand to pumping when I had to return to work because I only wanted you both to have the best. So through sore nipples, exhaustion, and juggling too many balls I added pumping to the routine and continued to push through the difficulty and exhaustion.

I was proud of my sacrifice, and became a walking billboard for breastfeeding and all things natural, no matter what society said about Black mothers and our ability to love and care for our children. I breastfed everywhere we went and shared my journey with anyone who would listen. I was a nursing and pumping machine for over a year with each of you. I often felt a sense of pride swell up inside when I opened the doors of the fridge or freezer to add more milk to my growing supply of white gold, as we called it. It grew so much I had to purchase my own lil' freezer to keep up with the flow. I had prayed for abundance and boy did God bless me with more than enough. Your dad was so proud that he showed everyone who came over what we had done for our boys. His love and support were integral during that time, allowing me to give you the best of me.

I knew what all the literature and reports said about breastfeeding and I was experiencing it for myself. You were never sick, rarely fussy and you were healthy, plump, happy and content, not to mention bright as ever! Now at 8 and 4, I reflect often on my days of breastfeeding with such fond memories of one of my greatest accomplishments as a woman, as a mom. I would do it over again without hesitation and I hope you as men and fathers can someday support your wives to do the same; to be *that mom*.

Love you both to the moon and back,

That mom! (Tiffany King-Clark Ph.d)

Breathe

In my mother's womb I was fully dependent on her wellbeing

She gave me life while showing its true meaning

As the years progressed doing it on my own became difficult

An asthma diagnosis but yet I stayed afloat

The time came when someone was dependent on me

He's alive and well but the focus was she

She was conceived in a more stressful environment

Years after him but still heaven sent

While in my womb she made a comfortable habitat

But preeclampsia made my body negatively react

I was dying but she needed me to live

28 weeks after implantation, and I had nothing else to give

My fervent mother stood praying by my side

A glance at the monitors and the baby

My true emotions I had to hide

I was scared my one task was to live for her

I failed and an emergency Cesarean had to occur

Pressed for time I was stretched on an operating table

I've seen my mom experience the same with my brother

So, I knew God was able

Able to deliver my daughter and me

From what doctors described a fatal end

Preparations were made

And the procedure was ready to begin

She was literally ripped from my uterus

And all I could do was wait for her cry

Instead, the doctor showed her to me--those big brown eyes

Preeclampsia was gone--her, my body denied

Now she had to live on her own without me as a guide

Oxygen for her was scarce and a machine was required

Weighing one pound

Her little lungs weren't taught how to respire

I was optimistic and started pumping milk to 'fatten' her up

Thoughts of me taking my little "No Name" home developed

Three days after her eviction from my body

I stood in disbelief

Several doctors surrounded her

But soon I'd experience a forever grief

Disconnected from her machines the doctor called the code

At 6:30 in the evening my happiness began to erode

With hands lifted....

My mother entered the room and began to pray

I stood filled with many emotions but I had nothing to say

She was gone, the life I thought I had given

She was gone, and selfish me, was still living!

The moment came for me to hold her for the first time

The cold I felt was unlike any cold felt in my lifetime

I couldn't take the pain so I gave her to my mother

Tears fell, my heart screamed, as I thought of her brother

I took her in my arms once more with such bravery

Thoughts crossed my mind...

That the ordinary person would say is crazy

I needed her to Breathe; I wanted her to Breathe

And if she couldn't do it on her own, it was left up to me

I placed my lips on hers with hopes of giving life

God Breathed into Adam

And he gave her to me-- it just seemed right

As I gently exhaled

I heard my breath pass through her little body

Softly rubbing her chest and repeating the exhales

I just wanted her to Breathe!

When asked what I wanted in this situation

My response was, "I want My baby back!"

She was gone and took a portion of me with her

And that's a fact

I needed her to Breathe, wanted her to Breathe

But instead, she left me...maybe it was her destiny

Feeling defeated, angry, and hurt

I bathed my precious daughter

I oiled her, clothed her

And within those three days fell deeply in love with her

I wrapped her in a warm blanket

My little "No Name" was ready

She made such an impact on my life in so little time

I finally named her Destinee

The time came for her body to forever leave my sight

I took pictures and captured that moment within my memory

Eventually I'll be alright

My beautiful Destinee forever you'll live within me

You're in heaven, now breathing and worshiping in His glory!

...And, Mommy Loves You!

 *Charlene Hendersen*

I Waited For You

I waited for you.

Long before I was old enough to conceive.

Ever since I was a little girl waiting for her mother to return from the wicked streets.

In the mornings I vowed to never allow you to wake not knowing where I was and wonder if I was coming back.

I waited for you.

Sitting in my elementary classrooms when I wanted a love of my own, suffering from a broken heart at a tender age.

I knew you were the only one that would intimately know the yearning of my heart, because you would listen to the rhythm it sang when it was overwhelmed with isolation and grief.

I waited for you.

In the hallways of my high school although I knew I was too young to bear a child at that moment.

I daydreamed about you and what it would be like to be your mother, and to love you unconditionally in the manner I longed to be loved as a child.

I yearned to greet motherhood head first and give to you what I was missing all of those years because you deserved it just as I had.

I waited for you.

On the bus ride home in Roseland when I saw acts of perverse child abuse daily I vowed to never hurt, abuse or neglect you.

But while I was waiting I needed to unlearn the dysfunction I was taught, to dismantle the mindset of neglectful and impoverished love.

I waited for you.

In my college classrooms as I prepared for your future and thirsted for knowledge that would make me a better person, more equipped to love you in a different way.

My heart's deeper desire was to break the cycle with you.

To unleash myself from the mental slavery elicited by the notorious warnings of the infamous Willie Lynch Letter; the dismantling of the Black family unit that would haunt generations to come:

That degree was dedicated to you long before you even existed, because it promised access to a better life.

You wouldn't be born into an uneducated family void of opportunity like I had been.

I waited for you as I secretly sat alone in the cold abortion clinic when I aborted a soul that would have been your sibling.

Although I wasn't "ready" to be a mother yet I wanted that baby more than I was ever willing to admit.

But, it was too soon I told myself, so I grieved for your sibling silently, but I kept living.

And I waited for you even more, this time content that I would be ready for you!

I waited for you.

Sitting on the toilet as I miscarried another soul and stared blankly into a sea of red and wondered what I'd done "wrong" this time.

But I knew your second sibling would protect you along your journey earth side, and I continued to wait.

Still not "ready," I thanked God for the miscarriage and picked myself up, and kept living, because after all, I was waiting JUST for you.

I waited for you.

As I sat in the doctor's chair and heard "You're pregnant!" just days before Mother's Day.

After all of the promises that I would one day be "ready," I was finally as "ready" as I needed to be

Because THIS time I opened my heart to God's whisper

After countless prayers of forgiveness and pleas, for you to be assigned to ME and enter this world safely.

Now you were finally gestating in my womb as I waited ever the more patiently for you.

I waited for you

After condoms, birth control and plan B you found your way to ME!

At 15 weeks I felt you kick for the first time and my heart grew ten times larger and ten times deeper to make room to love you.

39 long weeks and 4 days, you grew wonderfully in my womb as I prayed you were healthy and developing well.

Because part of me felt I wouldn't be able to keep you after what I'd done to the souls before you.

We read books, sang songs, and laughed endlessly passing time, just waiting to meet. We played games as we both simply waited for each other.

And, at last the wait was over and I would see your face soon...

My water broke at 7:04 am on January 8th

We bravely embraced 25 hours of natural labor and delivery.

I prayed to God fiercely the whole time that he would allow me to keep you.

I needed you.

And... the wait was far too long! 25 years is a long wait to meet your first child when you've always wanted a love of your own your whole life.

And, at last the wait *FINALLY* was over

Born 6 lbs. and 20 inches long, you greeted me with a cry that touched the deepest most untouched crevices of my heart and soul.

You nestled your little head into my breasts and latched effortlessly, like you had waited so long for that exact moment to be nourished outside of the womb by me.

As you suckled at my breasts, I knew we were a perfect match.

The first thing I noticed was that your birthmark mirrored mine.

Yours on the left side of your tummy, mine on my right!

Two identical hearts, the symbol of love!

And it was then that I knew the wait was not in vain. God smiled and said, "Wait no more beloved. I'm trusting you with this special soul, and she is made wondrously and perfect JUST for you."

 *J. T. B*

Memoirs of an Ebony Mother

Growing up with a single mother who worked very hard for her kids caused me to grow up tremendously fast. I was unsupervised from 7th grade on and I had a body of an 18 year-old, and no daddy to show me what true love was or how males should treat me.

My mother was young and had lost her mother shortly after she had children. I realized that losing her mother so early in her parenting journey left her with little to no emotional support, guidance and in serious grief and pain. My mother and I often didn't get along when I became a teenager. As a young mother herself she did not have the emotional support she needed and sadly, she didn't know how to give that to me. Many have said, it takes a village to raise a child, but for me, it was just my mother doing the best she could with what she had at the time.

Unfortunately, due to the circumstances of my upbringing, I never really got many lessons on being a woman. I received no guidance on how to even become a young lady. The importance of staying a child and maintaining my innocence wasn't instilled in me to provide a strong foundation. My mother's focus was making sure our bills were paid and we were fed and clothed. In that aspect, one would say I had an awesome childhood because I didn't want for anything. However, in retrospect, I now realize when a girl hits puberty she needs a father's reassurance and a mother's love in order to be well-rounded and balanced emotionally.

My father's absence left a void in my heart and unfortunately, I allowed older boys to attempt to fill that void. To get the attention of older guys I would fabricate about my age. In many ways, I found comfort in the embrace of guys who were older than me because it was attention from a male figure, attention I craved from my biological father. Their approval and love for me substituted my dad's love and approval, if only for a moment. This temporarily filled the empty space in my heart.

My mom had become a mother at age 16 and I became a mother at 17, but I was still a teenaged mother nonetheless. My son saved me though. I played grown for a very long time, but he was the first step in slowing me down. I was on the path to destruction even if I did love his father for a significant amount of time.

In our society, young girls are shamed for having children young or having sex at a young age, but the root of the problem stems far beyond the teenage mother or the pregnancy. To me, it was a generational cycle I vowed would stop with me and my family. The road to healing and recovery and disrupting the cycle started with educating my children about emotions and speaking out about how they were feeling. Pouring into them productively about the sacredness of their being was very important to me; the holy trinity, mind, body and spirit are critical to every human being. Rooting them deep into their history so they could stand strong and stay true to themselves was deeply important to my husband and I as well. Building up their self-esteems so they are confident about being themselves and ensuring that societal standards don't define them is our focus.

After having my son, I graduated from high school and made a conscious decision to go away to college. I had to get my son and myself away from the toxic area I grew up in. It really wasn't a place I wanted to raise my son in, and I knew an education was the way out of poverty for good. Although I went away to college the lessons in life didn't stop there and I continued to learn and grow as an individual. I attempted to have a happy little family, but there was nothing happy about it. My boyfriend at the time (who is now my husband) ran the streets and often allowed the sun to beat him home. I was completely devastated being alone all the time. It was painful to deal with being abandoned just so he could party with other college students. We argued a lot and our home was a very hostile environment. The atmosphere was not suitable for raising a child. I was depressed because I was all alone in college with a baby and no emotional support.

Thankfully, through the chaos, my son kept me grounded and gave me so much joy. It was through his happiness I was able to pull myself out of the darkness many days. While his father and I attempted to start patching our tattered and torn relationship, I conceived my second child when I was 22. My body completely rejected my second pregnancy and I gave birth prematurely. My precious baby was born at 28 weeks. During my pregnancy, my womb not only carried a baby, but I also carried the stress of a strained relationship. This was actually my second premature birth, but it was my first experience with giving birth to a baby so early that she had to be hospitalized and remain in the NICU for 3 months. After she was born, I battled with postpartum depression. I cried every night for those three months because it was so difficult to have a baby I could barely touch or bond with. Most days I found taking another breath hard to manage, and I could barely eat. I struggled with hormonal imbalances and craved the comfort of my baby, but I plastered a smile on my face to hide the river of tears I had cried in silence and behind closed doors.

I went through a destructive phase and completely destroyed my already tattered family. In turn, I was verbally abusive to my children's father. At some point, I decided our relationship was done and I would end it by dating someone else. I was completely numb to everything and I felt nothing. The naked truth is this is what I believe most mothers feel and can't really figure out how to say it. When you have children people don't really care too much about you as the mother, people want to hold and cuddle the baby. As a result, the smile I kept on my face meant to others I was okay. I lied when I filled out the depression questionnaires that were administrated during my NICU visits to see my daughter. After all I was a strong Black woman and could deal with what I was feeling, right? After all this I was supposed to be, strong, right? I was supposed to be strong enough to support my sick baby and parent my five year old through it all.

Growing up I was often told to just "suck it up," so showing signs of emotion were showing weakness in my eyes. I wasn't told that my emotions were my intuitions speaking to me, and as a human it was okay to show them because it was completely normal.

My kids will know about the intuition in emotions... That's a promise.

My boyfriend didn't understand what I was going through and neither did I. We argued constantly and eventually I left him, and he physically assaulted me. This was the final strike to my soul. I had experienced so many strikes to my soul throughout my life that had really never been healed.

It wasn't until I was drinking a pint or more of liquor a day that I finally realized I needed professional help. I was on a road to self-destruction. Unfortunately, the help I sought really didn't help me. When my therapist recommended I attend a meditation and yoga class, I took her up on the offer because at this point, nothing else seemed to improve my situation. I began to break through the fog and see things eventually shift for the better. This opportunity allowed me to heal from a great deal of trauma that I didn't even realize was there. Practicing yoga and meditation helped me to focus on what I needed to do to heal my children's trauma as well.

I learned to be gentle with myself and to design my life in a way that joy can always be found. I learned to pay attention to my own energy, and that allowed me to tune into my children's as well. My eyes became wide open to all the areas of life that had to be altered and changed in order to heal all of us. I started with my family, including my children's father. I had to heal that relationship because we had to break a whole lot of generational cycles. This process created a healthy space and fostered an environment that allowed me to fall back in love with the man he had become over the years.

Together we rebuilt our family and I was able to step both of my feet into motherhood and become who my children needed me to be. Both my husband and I have taken classes on ending the cycle of violence, the causes of trauma, and we have completed couples therapy. We had to renew and refresh our relationship because what we had before was unfixable if we continued on the same path. We have worked tremendously hard to do everything we can to produce thriving, healthy, happy, safe, and well-educated children. We wanted to change the way our children were being raised and focus on loving them and each other. In order to do so, we had to be the support we needed for each other.

Although I have always wanted children, becoming a mother young caused me a lot of pain. Not healing fully from my childhood trauma manifested itself within my adult life causing me to hurt the person I have loved the most for many years, and it also caused him to hurt me as well. We healed from our trauma together in order to be the mother, father, husband and wife we have always strived to be.

The saying, "When you know better, do better" is the motto for my family. The healing didn't stop at our relationship, it continued across all aspects of our lives. I just turned 26 and finally I was able to give birth to a healthy baby for my husband and my family. Changing my diet and healing my trauma allowed my womb to carry a baby full term for the first time. She has become my lotus baby and was a signal of the rebirth of my spirit in so many ways. After applying all the life lessons I had learned this far and the supplemental life classes I have taken, I feel like a whole woman now. I worked really hard recovering from my traumas. I have become very in tune with my energy and intuitions and the health of my womb. I was a mother before giving birth to my lotus baby but finally I was blessed into sacred motherhood and womanhood when she graced this earth.

Life continues as I navigate through my life as a woman, mother, and human being. Learning is a lifelong process. If you are not learning new lessons you are stagnant. Being a mother means you are responsible for passing all you know to your children so they can quickly learn the life lessons that you learned slowly.

 ***Rashena D. Johnson***

Watching Paint Dry Is GODLY

Watching paint dry is GODLY.
Because Black women are gods.
Because Black women are God.
Because GODS don't talk about paint drying.
Because paint is indeed drying.

Today the floor caved in.
I was not in the room.
Too busy painting bridges.
Bows wrapped around my wrists.
Mom said I was God's gift.

God sent.
But what does a God get?
A mouth full of glitter.
A fist full of stone.
Do not confuse my smile for content.
My hands are heavy.

Every time I sigh,
I choke on your sunshine.
So I stand in the shade.
Painting bridges.
Tying bows.
I cannot afford to drown in your sky.

<u>You see...</u> I dug deep into the depression, mental illness, angst and the vulnerability of Black women. I often compare depression to the feeling of watching paint dry instead of the sadness people often compare it to. Black women are so often told to be strong that we hide and tuck away anything that we see as "broken" or weakness in order to uphold this stigma, especially as mothers.

This in turn keeps us in a vicious cycle and until we open up and face these issues we will continue to be stuck in the cycle.

 *Tamera Larkins*

Enslaved by the Acts of Black Love: Black Love defines Beautiful Pain

"You did what?" He sternly shouted. He laced up his gloves and got into a Muhammad Ali boxing stance. He threw a fierce blow full of harrowing *"love"*. That powerful agonizing blow jabbed her right eye. She cried out, "Stop, not in front of the kids, please!!" But, nothing could stop him. The cocaine flowing through his veins strengthened his forceful blow and she just stood there. She just stood there and took each blow... She gave him an easy victory.

Go strong Black woman- you go! You loved hard, you allowed him to create a justified beautiful portrait of womanhood for your four beautiful young Black girls.

The portrait had beautiful vivid colors. Her melo-toned face had pretty blush purplish rosy eyes. Her cheekbones were covered in thunderous colorless raindrops. Her lips stained in a diverse color –dark-reddish maroon, and *"love"* outpoured from every angle of the portrait.

My sisters and I sat there and watched this painting rebirth itself repeatedly in different angles and shapes for about four years. The soaring cries grew louder and we embodied a lust full of expectations, of love that has enslaved our characters and tortured our hearts for many years. She championed the righteousness of abusive Black Love. Abusive Black Love! You bamboozled her soul and tortured her womanhood.

So I ask, strong Black woman how could you stand firm and tall, showered with the gold medals symbolizing abusive Black Love? Could it be the addictive heroine loving variegated with the false dreams and hopes of keeping a solid family unit together?

Black Love to me was just that; painful, weak-strong, shackled, and voiceless agony.

Empowered by Colorless Love

Witnessing and enduring this abusive Black love created a *beast* in me and I feared to love anyone other than my siblings and mother. Anyone who wanted to challenge my strength as a Black woman endured the painful, fearful yet abusive Black love that lingered in my heart and veins for years. In fact, I got into plenty of fights in school and lead riots that got me a name like no other; *"Gangster Nerd"*. I think that meant I was a smart and tough woman who didn't take any bullshit from anyone. But little did I know, the abusive Black Love I observed as a child would have an enormous impact on my existence and how I would function as an adult. What type of woman was I if I was feared and hard to love?

When I graduated from high school, I became more open with seeking the type of Black love that was not abusive. Thus, I allowed myself to leave my daunting environment and to excel as a powerful Black woman in a different social environment. I went away to college and emerged with different cultures. I didn't have "to be feared in order to be accepted," and I sure as hell didn't have to exert the taught defensive mechanisms of the agonizing Black Love to make me feel comfortable as a Black woman.

In college I joined a diverse sisterhood of women from all classes and races. I learned through the relationships with them that love looked different. Love was colorless. Black love is characterized by the experiences many Black families endured and each social class endured their own creeds of love. When I heard the unique experiences of Black Love that differed from my lived experience, I realized that I could create my own culture of Black Love. A culture of Black Love totally different from what I experienced growing up, but the first key to redefining my Black Love was to engage in self-love. But what was self-love? How could I obtain such a thing?

Self-Love was essential to developing my character. The act of caring for myself and understanding how to fulfill my needs and ultimately becoming an honorable woman was essential. I begin to love the skin I lived in, the kinky hair I was born with, and my desire to become enlightened about a distinctive form of Black love through courses about race and gender. I learned that the privileges I inherited from the abusive Black Love I grew up observing as a child were powerful! I had lived and experienced so much, that I was built indestructible and honorable at the same time. If I survived the abusive Black Love, I could definitely survive anything. Some people may not characterize my abusive Black love as privilege, but it's clear that experiencing such love supported the tough character and perseverance many people of my age lacked.

So I began my journey seeking out the new Black Love I wanted to embrace and share with future generations to come. On my quest for knowledge, I started to read about Black history through a sociological lens and theoretical framework. W.E.B DuBois enlightened me when he explained the history of the disfranchised Black families. I knew Black Americans had a rich history of enslavement, but I had very little to go off of to think critically about the different forms of social and physiological enslavements my ancestors encountered. I never thought about how keeping the family unit solid, especially after slavery, was crucial to the success of Black American families. This, then, made me think about the importance of a unified family regardless of the neglect and abusive circumstances. Abusive Black Love derived from this disfranchised ideal of wanting to keep tradition and to live by the societal expectations. This was indeed a painful reflection. At what cost was this unity?

We were given this painful culture of abusive Black Love, which ultimately and profoundly impacted the way in which we functioned and interacted with one another as Black Americans. So I decided to adopt some of the middle class morals I learned as an elite college student. I began speaking elaborately and thinking analytically about starting new traditions to stimulate my thinking about the Black Love I so eagerly yearned.

I experienced different cultures as I traveled across the world and engaged in meaningful conversations around race and social class. I wrote challenging 30-page papers using historical research to reshape my own thinking about Black culture and Black love and finally came up with a definition of Black Love.

My new definition of Black love wasn't as dark as I experienced as a child and a teenager. I came to realize that Black Love is a way of loving others and appreciating sisterhood. It is simply an act of being eager to learn from, prosper with, and love those around me. It is not allowing any man to play a crucial role in identifying who I am as a woman. Being strong in Black Love meant to stand firm and not take the physical and social-emotional abuse from any weak character. It is fighting for the civil rights of those who are voiceless. Black love is leading the blind and fighting to keep families united as one. Black love is walking down an unpaved self-created path to socially mobilize in order to create a better life for the future generations to come.

So I ask again, strong Black woman how could you stand firm and tall showered with the gold medals symbolizing abusive Black Love? I stand strong with gold medals symbolizing my right to love and become fearless.

However, the ideal of a powerful Black man (or any man for that matter) being included in my definition of Black love was absent. Here I found myself again, "enslaved by the acts of Black love" because I could not fit a man into such a beautiful picture. I was haunted by my past experiences, and the absence of a man's role in Black Love made my definition of Black Love invalid.

To incriminate oneself in the act of love is to physiologically infest hatred on the opposite sex and relive the pains of my UPBRINGING of abusive Black Love.

After graduation I went back to my hometown. As soon as I re-entered my initial culture of abusive Black Love, I begin to relive some of those same experiences in my adulthood. I begin to lose everything including the aspects of self-love and Black love I worked hard to develop. I began dating men who weren't of pure quality. Those relationships with the men I dated did not allow me to thrive in a positive Black Love. I struggled to live in the Black Love I had envisioned for myself during self-exploration. It was easy to fall victim to the abusive Black Love I encountered growing up because my definition of Black Love did not explain the role of a man within the Black Love framework. The shackles on my thinking of Black Love prevented me from understanding how to open up and love a man.

The men I dated physiologically abused me as I allowed for them to cheat and emotionally beat down my character. I by no means want to pretend I was innocent and faithful during the relationships because I cheated. I constantly justified my actions for engaging in such relationships and it all made sense to me. My self-love had flown away and I had found myself caged in with abusive Black Love yet again. I found myself strong as a leader and weak as a woman.

Then I got pregnant and made the decision to birth a powerful child of Black love, even if it meant I would have to raise him or her as a single parent. I was nervous. Four months into my pregnancy, the father of my unborn child began to physiologically and emotionally abuse me. I had nightmares about being that *strong Black woman* my mother represented as a defeated victim. There was no way I could allow for this abusive Black Love to enter the bloodstream and soul of my unborn young leader so I decided to take this journey of parenting of my own. It was time to utilize that key to unlock the shackles off my mind, body and soul. I could no longer be enslaved by the acts of abusive Black Love for the sake of my unborn child; the cycle had to stop here.

For many long nights, I prayed and prayed without ceasing. I asked God to give me the strength to be strong enough to raise my child with a more positive Black Love, like the one I'd re-envisioned and then lost as I returned home. I read to her every morning and every night as she rested in my womb. I read the research papers I authored in college and reread historical research that kept me grounded in the faith and a new Black Love. I listened to

Jazz and Blues music. I ate healthy green foods and fruits to nourish her growing brain. I even invested in the best prenatal pills I could find to ensure my child had a wonderful brain development journey. I exercised both in and outdoors to keep my body in stellar shape and prepare for giving birth. I did just about everything I thought would support my notion of Black love.

I finally took care of myself in order to take care of the unborn child gestating in my womb. However, the missing male presence created a little anxiety. How strong can a woman be without a man? I wanted a family- a loving caring significant other who would be there for both my child and I. But what did this look like? I was willing to figure out what it *should* look like and forgave the father of my child and allowed myself to relive the painful physiological abuse over again in an effort to include him in our daughter's life. My weakness prevailed once again and my thinking was enslaved by the acts of abusive Black Love for the last time.

Her Birth Re-birthed My Black Love

After twenty-seven hours and exactly fifty-six minutes of labor, I birthed a new life into this world. I gained the strength like no other woman (well I thought). I was a super woman for birthing a beautiful baby girl. I was untouchable, unstoppable even... I saw those beautiful eyes and finally for the first time in life, Black Love, true Black Love existed. Not the shackled agonizing abusive Black Love I was accustomed to, but a Black Love that made me stand up and say enough is enough. I am the mother and leader of this young soul. I decided to leave the father of my child alone forever and no longer pursue a romantic relationship! After leaving the hospital I asked him to pack his bags and co-parent with me.

He did just that and we co-parented for about six months before I became a single parent. Not surprised, but the birth of this innocent child gave me a new life myself. Now my Black Love is within her and all of my experiences I endured to gain this love made plenty of sense. I was built to conquer love and raise a powerful Black woman. I, as a role model for her, will never fall short to abusive Black Love. Raising her to love the skin she is in and to always think critically about the world she lives in is our Black Love. Teaching her to follow her dreams and never fall victim to the voiceless agony is our Black Love. Teaching her that life has challenges that she will conquer is our Black Love.

My role is to inspire, uplift and deliver this revived Black Love. So Black woman, what is glorified righteousness? It is Black Love. It is to believe in one's own self and to overcome the obstacles of societal barriers. It is looking into my Leah's eyes and saying, "Baby, you are great!" It is leading by example and encouraging the new generation to lead and conquer love. It is opening up one's heart to love again after all of this pain. More importantly, it is not being enslaved by the acts of Black love but redefining Black love as it fits the heart of my existence and new creation.

Dear Black Love,

I knew I could find you. And there you were staring me in the eyes at 6:46 A.M on the 26th of April. Shackles are unlocked and I am free. My portrait defines a strong un-bruised woman with healed bones of sorrow.

Sincerely,

 **Shanika Star Bridges-King**

Woman as Mother Part I

Bet you know more than one

Woman or mother

Came from one

Always had one around

As you growed up

Think you done growed up

Live a few years and let life happen

Watch you'll bleed

The need to grow up some more

Or die trying

To imagine you good

And got it all under control

Woman and mother

You were once a little girl

Not many dolls to practice on

No siblings till later on

Right before

Unsure stages of womanhood

Were drenched by unanswered questions

As she stuffed her ears with the fear of hearing

"Let her learn the hard way!"

Well now it has been spoken into existence

Young girl growing up agrees

So the hard way it is

In every young girl

Is a fragile frame and foundation

For Woman as Mother

She must live

Why let only experience

Aid in the haphazard gathering

Of information

We watch her let it ride when she's denied

The ability to ask

Or the option to think

And that matters

How else will she discover and value

The importance of all creations

And the current of time

Now she is acting out of character

As if she has accepted

The ideas and identity imposed

By strangers from the outside

Billboards, newspapers, TV shows and radios

Lacking validity and still having impact

Can she ignore messages that interrupt her smiles?

And say that teenage pregnancy is on the rise,

3 in 5 will contract an STD,

Black men will die by the age of 18,

Hypertension this

And, prison rates that,

Disproportionately affects people who love living in

The brown skin given to them by

.....Woman

Without plan she traveled a path

Living out loud

Allowing men in,

They believe they increased her

While they diminished her innocence

Grown Girl Now becoming a Fake Woman

Suffers and encounters itchy situations

Miscarriages on El-Trains before her rites of passage

Left to write about nights she didn't have the courage to read

Relatives whispered and carefully collected her pain

Placed it under a rug that was vacuumed daily

She sat and brushed her own hair, to burn

Which women had littered with nonchalant words,

And clichés dressed up like concern.

After the bath there was no more words, no more life

Could she ever erase the pain?

It was like the Black outline of the coloring page

From a book that belonged to a little girl she left behind.

Six pregnancies and three living births,

Woman as Mother now is she

With or without the necessary preparation

Now it's lights, camera, and action anyway

She is responsible for the lives, experiences, choices of two males

She calls them "The Boys"

She shares her whole world with them

They grew food in the garden and the streets were in the kitchen

They were trapped in their environment

Children who cannot pack up and leave

Smeared by society's expectations

Regardless of their test scores, removed from class for asking questions

Conferences filled with statements like, "but they speak so well"

She fights for a different standard against the system and their rules

Curfew, drinking age, dating, fashion, music and roles

A world with a nasty mouth waits to consume her children without condolences or remorse

Woman as Mother, never thinks she has to prepare to lose

Who she sat on her lap and fed from her breasts

She never saw it coming, she wasn't facing the wall

The one that someone put the writing on, even when her 4 year old said

"I'm going to die and go to heaven to see God....and it's okay."

An unsorted message

Then he was shot

Just two weeks after turning 16

He was shot...

She lives every day now unsure of what life means

Now she is one of those Mothers

Ever met "The Mothers?"

Those mothers who walk through the community and pray on corners

For the shooting to stop to anyone who would listen and especially each other

Their daily walk is without a child on both sides

One child in the prison system and the other child in the ground

After having received the news, something like... "It's a boy"

Except this time it was that her child was not alive anymore

Or a recorded call you press 1 or 2 for

Who decided this shit was part of the plan?

For millions of women to be without child had to be this system created by man

No way to dress it cute, but to accept it as truth

And if the smell wasn't so foul, then all "The Mothers" could shed their tears and flood this world out

As the wind continues its business

They continue to be with the *ifs* and demand from the seeds of other women

No violence and some healing, then they stand again

Code Red, with signs to the streets on the sidewalks

Come together with ones from the other side

To listen and simply just to talk

Women as Mothers

 *Princess Titus*

A Work In Progress

I woke up this morning feeling like I couldn't catch my breath. The weight of the world was so heavy that I was starting to feel my back breaking. I had to tell myself you've been through worse and you have crawled through more shit and still managed to come out clean on the other end. But damn, Mama needs to be held sometimes too.

After the death of my Grandfather, my divorce and running away from my abusive ex I found myself extremely depressed. Walking around the world in somewhat of a fog because I felt alone. No one has time to feel loneliness or depression I have children to raise. I come from a long line of strong Black women and being depressed is for the weak, at least that's how I felt. So, "push through it girl" is all the self-talk I could offer myself to hold things together.

I immersed myself into my children and my work. I started the battle for Mothers and babies. My day started with me getting up sending emails, making phone calls and working on my organization. Then making meals for my children and homeschooling them. Wake up the next morning, rinse and repeat. This continued on for almost three years. People would tell me, "you have to find time for yourself". Damn, that was such an annoying statement. Do you think I need you to remind me that I exist? Come on people I'm 30+ years old, I have known I exist for a long time. I don't want time to myself. Finding time for myself meant I had to deal with the pain that I was feeling and I didn't care to deal with. I want to focus on helping everyone else. Perhaps if I help enough people the pain I was feeling would just vanish by it, leave without me having to do any work.

I sat down with a friend as she told me how much I helped her overcome so much pain. I had some of my breastfeeding clients go out of their way to call me to say I was such a "Godsend". Sighs, no matter how much help I was for others, no matter how big the smiles were on my children's faces, I still found myself up nights crying or watching old episodes of Judge Judy because I couldn't sleep. I'm so tired of hurting, I must do more work is what I constantly told myself. I'm not busy enough, I have too much time to think about how much I was hurting. So, I dug harder into my business life. Now instead of just running my organization, homeschooling my children and helping take care of my Mom who was injured in a car accident, I became the President of a Black Mothers Breastfeeding organization and started to have community meetings at my home, because the work had to be done. Then he walked in the door. Holy shit I'm in trouble now! Tall, dark skinned, super intelligent, educator, good father, strong and kind. Laughing, "yeah right he can't be all that" is what I told myself. Then we talked and talked and talked and talked some more. He scared the hell out of me. I had been, abused, belittled and underappreciated by the last man I entrusted my heart to. There was no way in the hell I was going through that again. But he is such a good man. I know what I'll do, I'll find him a woman so he can fall in love and get married. Then he won't be on the market for me any longer. Laughing, yeah I know it sounds nuts but trust me I have weighed all the options and that's the only one that made sense to me. I don't need anyone around that would make me think I could actually find real love in the crazy world.

Wednesday night I sat home alone for the first time in 3 years. I washed clothes, I mopped the floors, I tried to watch a movie but it was too stale. I hated being alone with my own thoughts, I almost called my Mother to tell her I changed my mind about my children staying the night. I distracted myself with the lives of others. I got on Facebook and started to read what all my Facebook friends were up to. Yes, you guessed it. He was online and we started talking. I asked him over and just laid in his arms and cried. I honestly can't remember the last time I trusted anyone enough to allow them to see this side of me. He held me all night. I laid there listening to this sound of his heartbeat and he sounded like music. He snored loud enough that it made the bed vibrate. It was just what I needed, to feel safe and cared for. From that point forward we spent a lot of time together. He would come over for dinner and we would talk about everything from the astrology to dirty diapers. It felt like I had made a real friend. The closer we got the more I feared what could happen if I allowed myself to be happy. So, I started asking tons of questions. Turns out he was involved with at least 5 women. Laughing, I knew it was too good to be true. No man was as kind and understanding about the feminine mind like he pretended to be. Let me pull back a little because I don't want to get caught up in this type of drama either.

Back to focusing on my work and taking the attention off him. Things at work were growing at an impressive rate. Then I experienced the most frightening thing in my life. I had a stroke. What? Me? I am a Professional Fitness Trainer, a Yoga Instructor, a nutritionist, how could I have a stroke? I don't even have high blood pressure, I don't even allow myself the time needed to think about me enough to even be stressed. How could I have a stroke? I laid in that hospital for about 24 hours and couldn't move, couldn't talk, I couldn't do anything but lay there and think. Isn't it amazing how the body works? You try to avoid thinking about you and your body and put you on your ass and all you have is time to think about yourself.

That stroke changed my life. I woke up the following morning feeling like nothing ever happened to my body but I could see the difference. I wanted to be in love, I wanted to experience my own happiness, I wanted to get married again. I was informed in the hospital I was pregnant. My life really changed in the blink of an eye. I'm 35 years old and had a stroke and now I'm about to become a Mother of three (3) children. It took me months to tell this man who had become my friend and my go to person that we were having a child. But he took it really well. He just said to me, "okay well we will figure out how to make this work". Things were unfolding in ways that I never thought they would but he was really turning out to be the kind man I believed him to be. I was getting use to the idea of Mothering another child and trying to figure out what co-parenting would look like for us. I didn't have to worry about co-parenting with my older children because their Dad was in the wind. All the prep work was for nothing because other forces were at work and this child was not allowed to come home with us. After we worked to elevate our child so he could walk with our ancestors, things with him started to change. He didn't trust any words I ever spoke. I know I took things hard but what was going on with him? Was he angry? Did he regret being with me? Sighs, I was starting to question myself. I was hurting but how did I release the pain when my go to person spoke like I was an interruption in his day? Just like I feared, he was gone out of my life. Again, I was all alone.

I looked up one day and months had gone by. I attended a community meeting and there he was. But something was different. He looked sad, he didn't sit with the same type of confidence I was used to seeing. I went over and spoke with him. He seemed like he had the weight of the world on his shoulders. I asked him to come over to my home so we could talk. He cried and cried, in the few months since we last spoke he had fallen in love. He talked about how much she hurt him. I wanted to hold him yet I wanted to scream because I wasn't ready to hear him talk about another woman like this. We tried to restore our friendship but all we did was hurt each other daily. I felt like I had gotten into a domestic violence relationship. He would lash out at me, I would lash out at him. We were hurting each other every chance we could get. The emotional abuse was out of control. He would tell me about all the men he saw me with in the community that he thought I was sleeping with, and he would tell me about the women he was sleeping with. I couldn't figure out why I couldn't let him go. Then I get pregnant again. There we were with the most dysfunctional relationship I had ever heard of and we are bringing another child into the world.

My pregnancy was stressful. After trying to be in a committed relationship, all we really did was put the final nails in the coffin of us. He told me he had been here before. Lied to about a child being his and he wasn't dealing with that again. He was gone in the wind too and here I stood awaiting the birth of our Sun with Dad in the wind again. Damn, I can't believe this had become my life. I'm pregnant and I had to Mother my other children through tears. I recall getting up in the middle of one of our homeschool lessons to cry in a room separate from my older children. When our child was the ripe old age of one week old we sat in a clinic getting a paternity test. The first few months of our Suns life was stressful. I felt like I wanted to just hide under a rock. But of course we couldn't let things end there. We had to ensure that we hurt each other one last time. We got into another relationship with each other, yet again and we walked around each other on pins and needles. I worried about saying anything that would turn into an argument and I could see that he wanted to say something but he held it in as well. After a few more months of hurting one another I finally gave up.

For the first time in a long time, I chose me. I have been taking care of Moon for the first time since my Grandfather died in 2005. I still have my moments though when I forget about myself. When I see him with the children and I see how much they love him, I feel bad that we allowed things to get so bad. I am a work in progress and it feels good to finally be number one (1) on my to-do list.

Afrykan Moon, President of Breastfeeding Mothers Unite and Creator of "The History of My Chocolate Milk" Documentary

Through the Pain

Introduction: The journey of teenage motherhood is a wonderful and life-changing experience that can also be painful. It is a journey filled with self-doubt, nay-sayers, destroyed confidence, and giving of every ounce of yourself. There has been many times when I have been in situations where I thought I had given all that I had just to surprise myself and miraculously muster up more to give to my children. My journey as a pregnant teen to having another child almost nine years later is one that nobody but God could have seen me through.

Welcome My Diamond: At the tender age of 17, I gave birth to a baby girl. What was supposed to be a celebrated experience of giving life was a shameful disaster. This is what I was told by so many people. I was told some very disgusting things that destroyed my confidence. I was told my life was over; that I was only a statistic, to abort my child, and that I had singlehandedly ruined my life. But I proclaimed that God was the author of my story and in the midst of adversity a *Diamond* was born. With the birth of my daughter, I made a personal goal to prove I was not a statistic, and my child would not grow up in poverty like her father and I had.

Not a Statistic: What I once knew to be love turned into hate rapidly. The person I once adored stooped so low to even spit in my face. The person who I thought was the love of my life, my soon to be husband, the father of my child had become happy and content while my soul was dying. I was on every form of public assistance there was. We lived in the heart of the ghetto with roaches and the words "you're just a statistic" continuously echoed over and over in my head.

There had to be more to life than this. I had to leave him where he was and elevate higher; being stagnant was not an option for me, because I had a daughter depending on me. I graduated high school number 8 of 275 students and Vice President of the National Honor Society with my 2 year-old Diamond, and set off for college. However, I couldn't go far because I needed help with my daughter. To make ends meet, I had to go to school full-time, work part-time, be a mom full-time, and manage the upkeep of my apartment. Yet seeing her walk, hugging her, spending days in the mall, trips to the nail shop with her, her falling asleep while I did my homework, and her running to me when I came home from work made it all worthwhile.

My daughter was three years old when she started to learn gang signs. That same year I had to get an order of protection against her father. He had broken into our house and put a knife to my neck, "cause if he couldn't have me no one could." He was seriously stalking me, breaking into my house, and scaring off all the guys I attempted to date. That next year, my daughter was playing in the park and I heard gunshots. That familiar sound made my heart stop beating. Right before my eyes, the park was being shot at while kids were playing. The worst experience any mother will ever face is their child being in danger, and having to explain that to your child. One evening we came home and our house had been robbed. Diamond looked at me and said, "mommy we in danger." As those words escaped my first-born's mouth, my heart literally shattered into pieces. At that moment I vowed even if I had become a "statistic," she would not be one.

Against many odds, I graduated from college with a B.S in Business Administration and started grad school courses online. At this point, my daughter was going to first grade and I moved to a more secure apartment complex on the east side of the city. I thought life was finally settling down and I know if I held fast, in just two more years I'd be a Certified Public Accountant. With this qualification, I'd be more financially secure, and my child would be safe.

One semester away from graduating grad school I started to become reluctant about becoming an Accountant. I was informed that my child couldn't read, and was performing behind in almost every subject. I focused so much on providing the basic necessities and my own educational goals, that I neglected her education. Ultimately, I finished school with an MBA and set my focus on my child catching up. We struggled because I didn't know how to teach a child, and she just shut down. I could tell she wasn't confident and she was frustrated because she wanted to make good grades. The school system had just closed her school, and I wasn't getting the support that I needed for her to succeed. The bank I was working at was undergoing a major change in leadership, and job security became an issue for me. I got a new job, still working in commercial banking doing the same kind of work just for a bigger company.

The Move: After a few months of being on the job we moved again, and I put my daughter in a level one school. Finally, we were both happy. Her second grade teacher requested I get her eyes checked and it just so happened she was nearsighted, which had affected her ability to read and write all this time. After receiving new glasses, her grades started to improve in every subject.

I had fallen in love again, however just as the relationship began to go south, I'd found out I was pregnant again by my new lover who was facing a case and jail time. I decided the stress added by being with this man was too much to bear and I had to cut ties with him immediately. He moved out while I was at work. When I returned I found that he had stolen some things from me. Less than a week later he was in jail.

I was pregnant, mother of an eight-year-old, and on the other side of town isolated from all of my family and friends. To add to my load, I lost my job. Slowly but surely, life as I knew it was crumbling fast. Looking at my daughter and my growing stomach, I knew giving up was not an option. At 20 weeks my daughter and I went to see if the baby was developing appropriately and to determine the gender. Upon seeing the ultrasound, Diamond shrieked, "Look, I see our baby," and at that moment I knew somehow everything would be just fine.

When I was eight months pregnant with my angel, his father, was released from jail. I wanted nothing to do with him but he convinced me that him not being a part of the child's life was not good for either of us. We fought about names, him signing the birth certificate, and him being there when *Gabriel* was born. I gave in to him and we decided to slowly work toward having a relationship. Two weeks later he just flat out up and disappeared, blocked me on Facebook, and changed his number altogether.

My Angel: While I was giving birth on Sweetest Day, a Midwestern holiday created to celebrate love, I found out that the father of my child was on a mini vacation with another woman after begging me for a second chance at our relationship. Despite this harsh news, I held my son tightly and loved on him. My daughter was in the hospital waiting room when he was born. When I watched her hold him life was complete again. With the two of them present in my life, I loved on a whole new level. This was a love unlike anything I'd ever experienced.

Once released from the hospital, I was by myself. I got in my car with my newborn prince, my angel, drove to pick up my older child, and the three of us went home. I had no time to rest and no time to heal properly. In fact, I was dropping my daughter off at school and picking her up in addition to filling out job applications the very next day. There was nobody but me to tend to my babies or handle my responsibilities. My daughter had been struggling so hard with school, that I couldn't allow her to miss a single day. The third grade was one in which she couldn't fail due to state testing and tracking. In addition to this, I was still out of work so I had to find a job soon, my unemployment was running out, but my bills didn't stop.

At two-months-old, my son still has not met his father. He was too busy living his life and proclaiming, "If I wouldn't be with him, he wouldn't be a part of my son's life." To say the least, this has been a very difficult and heart breaking journey for me. I know more things are going to happen, there will be more pain but I would not redo any of it. My heart has never been so full or happy in my life because of my children. Gabriel chuckled today for the first time, and Diamond's eye lit up when she said, "oh mom you heard that?"

When you become a mom your personal agenda no longer matters. If it weren't for motherhood, I would not know what true love was. Motherhood has not been easy by far, but it has definitely been the most rewarding experience of my life. Being a mother is a very challenging experience that you have to learn as you go because there definitely isn't a manual. There are many nights you may cry, there are many times you may feel like giving up, there are many times you may feel like your best is just not good enough, and there are many times you may feel life is just not fair. However, the reward for your trouble, heartache, and pain is so great. Seeing your children happy, smiling, giving you hugs means you have favor with God because he entrusted you with life, and the sense of being more than a conqueror; a champion.

 *Tesha Harvey*

What Happens When All Optimism Fades? / Do What You Gotta Do

What happens when all optimism fades?
When the luck ends short like nipped braids?
When you've given your whole soul
And altered your old ways,
To the fault of your own
What you've sown just don't pay.
No returns on the loans of old days.
Been in the zone, eyes on the throne
Rising and grown
Prize in the pupils of your eyes
What you've shown is the determination,
So much motivation
So you're showing patience, but the hope is fading thin
Only so long we can wait before the jaded nature wins
Your spirit's weak as paper plates, the extra weight will
cave us in
Placing stems of doubt, making damage irreparable
Like cerebellum lacerations, separable navigation
Of the body and the mind, several destinations
When they're no longer combined.
Mentally exhausted
Maybe physically you're fine.
Spiritually the energy exuded leaves you crying...for
days.

What happens when all optimism fades?
Do what you gotta do; shoot to become suma cum laude.
Assume that soon that opportunity's gotta come
knocking.
To shoot for the moon the view has gotta be telescopic.
The proof is in the stew, but brewing is always a process

Do what I do, and stay true to the truth, so regardless
Of the few who choose to boo from the pews when I'm
talking,
I stay astute, salute and do what they hate,
I'm A. C. Lewis the truest prophet to spit since Elijah.
It's obvious.

 **A. C. Lewis**

Missing Piece

Who am I? Am I the woman with an abused little girl trapped inside? Am I that heartless little girl who hopes that one day she will be loved unconditionally? Who am I? From everything I've endured throughout my childhood one would say, "Move on and look beyond the hurt and pain", while others may rejoice in my strength practiced throughout childhood leading to adulthood and be inspired by my tenacity to overcome the hardship. But, who am I really? Pieces of a mended and scarred me make up my being, but I declare, I am a strong African-American woman and like many women of my race, I was tormented by difficult times, but yet overcame each and every trial and tribulation. Overcoming my obstacles was a tough, yet liberating time in my life. I sought counseling and became comfortable in my own skin. I learned how to love myself and in return love someone else for showing me that despite my upbringing, I had a lot to share with the world. Being able to be open in my counseling sessions allowed me to tap into my inner feelings in which taught me how to feel genuine love for another human being. Upon becoming a mother I reached back into my past sessions and it allowed me to exude unconditional love to this new person that I was now responsible for.

As a little girl slowly my life began to shatter. I was fortunate enough to have my father present in the house but unfortunately he chose drugs and alcohol over his "first born." Why didn't he love me the way a dad should love his precious little girl? Why did he continually choose everything and everyone over me? I watched my friends bond with their fathers and I yearned for that same love and affection from my own. After all, that is the natural human response, especially for a young girl. Sometimes I would wonder how and why he would praise me in the presence of others while telling me "fuck you" and "I'll beat yo' ass" when I mentioned my hurt and my expectations of him as my father. I just needed him to see me as his precious baby girl but instead he overlooked me causing this missing piece, this void in my heart in need of mending. By having my dad absent in my life and not showing me what a father/daughter bond entailed, it made me feel empty. Upon having my first born I promised myself that I would be a better parent to my daughter Kala than my parents were to me. Having a father who lacked emotion and parenting skills made me think about who I wanted as the father of my children. I was soon on the search for a man who valued family, showed empathy and most importantly wasn't afraid to love.

I was raised by my paternal grandparents but prior to living with them I lived with my mother, and the atmosphere was no different from being with my father. My mom was gone all the time but while I was home with my older sister a family friend started molesting us. At the tender age of seven, "I-Man" was in full control of us. Sadly, those long gruesome nights haunted me and I had no one to turn to who would protect me. I was held captive in what I called home while a horrible man took advantage of my sister and myself. I felt like I had no one in my corner and no one loved me enough to stop this from happening to me. Soon I was moved to a shelter exclusively for homelessness. The shelter consisted of 3 families or more to a room. Upon arriving to the shelter I asked my mother how long were we going to be staying here and she stated "until they find us somewhere to go, but you can't tell your grandparents where we are staying because they will try and take you from me"! I didn't say a word; I followed the rules because I enjoyed being with my mother even though I was unhappy where we were residing at the time. Every morning we would wake up and get dressed and go down to the community kitchen and eat the shelters lack luster breakfast. We would then go into a community room to play with toys along with the other children. I cried every day because I wanted my own home away from strangers and the nasty smell of the shelter. Despite the environment and the nasty selection of food, I was at peace due to the fact that I was under the supervision of my mother and no one would harm me anymore. Ironically, while sitting there in the homeless shelter a news special was broadcasted showcasing me and people like me. Upon viewing, my grandparents and father rushed to the rescue of my sister and I, and finally I found happiness, but little did I know that if would only be temporarily. Happiness was when I saw my father with my grandparents and thoughts of him repenting and finally wanting me, his baby girl, ran through my mind. Instead he distanced himself from me and thoughts of him receiving me with open arms were just a dream.

While at my grandparent's house, my sister and I shared a room next to their room and at that very moment I felt loved and safe again. Soon after being settled in, my newly released from prison cousin moved back into the house and everything changed. I remember being molested again almost every night while living in my new home but didn't understand why. Why was this constantly happening to me again? Was this the norm? I was tortured by seeing him every day and him fondling me every night, but I remained silent... Silent about his abuse... I remained silent because thoughts of again not having a home crossed my little mind and I was afraid of what would happen if I disclosed what was being done to me... Silent because no one would believe me. I was my father's own child and my father was a habitual liar; someone who would steal and dismantle relationships throughout the family, and being a product of him, I feared my voice would not be heard or be taken seriously. I didn't want to be labeled as the family 'trouble maker,' so I held my silence for many years. It wasn't until I was in my junior year of college that I uttered a word about being molested. While growing up, I literally felt as if I had no one to run to, not even my father or other male figures in my family. In the Black community it is known that the less people know your family business the better, or as most people from the inner city would say "snitches get stitches!" It was well known that what goes on inside the four walls of your home stays within these four walls, but the problem was that I was the only one who knew what was happening to me. Being raised to believe that things are better left unsaid had me trapped, and it's problematic to allow abuse to happen or be pushed under the rug.

       Once again I was broken, and shattered into more pieces. I felt alone and embraced my newfound anger from within. Love was just a phase that didn't exist in my world. I knew nothing of emotions towards the opposite sex because I had been forced to numb myself as a coping mechanism. I even avoided looking men in the eyes because I grew to view men as predators and I was full of rage. Sex was awkward, and trusting a man seemed nearly impossible; the anger consumed me. I was absolutely furious all the time! My innocence was stripped away and revoked at a very young age and sorrowfully I could never restore those years. When I think about it, I never had the luxury or experiencing sex on my own, or at my own pace, but was forced to endure such evilness against my will, and that changed me to my core. Looking back I am still broken from the situation but God strengthens me in the darkest hours and at my weakest moments!

Years later while enrolled in a widely known state university I met my husband. Upon us meeting, this new emotion captivated my very being and for once I was in a reciprocal loving relationship. I couldn't explain this feeling but I concluded this was true love! He was unlike any man I've seen in my lifetime and for the first time ever, a man saw me; he saw all of me and respected my body and this was a new feeling! He was the total opposite of my father and I loved everything this man exuded. This fairytale love turned into hate when I realized my guard was being chiseled away, and I had to be vulnerable. I didn't like that feeling because of my past. How could someone love me, the once abused little girl? Who told him to love me through all my hurt and pain? Didn't he know I was incapable of loving anyone since all I had ever experienced in life was hate? But he didn't give up even when I pushed him away. "Should I let him in? I wonder if he's just trying to use me like every other man in my life." These thoughts constantly raided my mind. Scared from the possible outcome of true happiness I began to lash out, hitting him through every disagreement. It liberated me to finally be able to show anger and emotion when I felt that I was being wronged by a man, but it only hurt me more because this was the man who tried to love me unconditionally. My life was an emotional roller coaster and cynically I pulled him along for the ride. Before leaving me, he pleaded with me to seek help and I knew in his tone, a change was imperative. He never walked away, he never belittled me, and he showed me such a genuine love... unlike my father. It was at that point I realized I had to seek counseling and finally face the past.

I sought professional help and help from my Lord Jesus Christ; change in me is but an understatement. My Lord has fully restored me and blessed me in such a way that I can't explain! My past missing pieces are now complete with my loving and successful husband and my two beautiful children. Although I didn't have a relationship with my father, my daughter is blessed with an affectionate father that is actively showing her how a man should treat and appreciate a woman. And my son is watching first-hand how to be a man. Through everything I've encountered God has shown love and mercy when he blessed me with my own family. My father is just a man and I'm his seed, and I'm content with the fact I'll never be his "little girl." Does this hurt—yes but I'm blessed to witness my daughter not having a missing piece like me. She's daddy's little girl and I'm proud to say my once missing piece ended with me and not my offspring. With them the cycle will be broken and I love them unconditionally.

Lakeyia D. Johnson

Growing Past Myself for the Life of my Children

I have been a Mother since the age of seventeen. Needless to say, I still had a ton of growing to do and wouldn't know for years later how my childhood experiences would influence the way I raised my children. I was very dismissive of their feelings and experiences, which carried on with an undertone of "You'll survive."

Once I found out I was pregnant with my first son my journey was almost immediately rocky. I told my mother about twenty-four hours after I found out via a written letter. Writing has always been the best way for me to get all I need to say out. She was so distraught that when I came home from school I discovered she didn't go to work and she was still in her gown. With this sight, I immediately knew the conversation would be interesting to say the least.

I was sitting in a chair in her bedroom when she began to interrogate me about how "IT" happened. She sort of listened to my answers, but mostly just screamed about how I did this on purpose and proceeded to tell me how much of a whore I was. Oh yea, I was a few "b*tches" too. Every degrading name that escaped her lips felt like a stab in the heart. This was my MOTHER. I was a GREAT child. I just had sex. She knew I was sexually active. I asked for birth control and she ignored me. I used condoms. She called me a liar. The final blow came when she told me I was GOING to have an abortion. She didn't ask if I wanted to, but she assured me I was GOING to have one by force. This was the first fight I would ever have for the life of my son. I informed my mother that I simply would not have an abortion. I just refused to do it. I made the decision to have sex and I wasn't going to stop the growth of my child because it's timing was off by the standards of myself, my mother, and whoever else felt disdain about my pregnancy.

My mother and I didn't talk for months. My Aunt was staying with us at the time and she was the one who communicated between the two of us. I didn't have health insurance and that coupled with the delayed communication meant no prenatal care for a long while. Every stage of this pregnancy I was forced to grow a little more for the sake of my child. I signed myself up for Medicaid and scheduled my first appointment.

Each day I was ill I pushed forward to attend school anyway. Then, I was admitted to the hospital for preterm labor. From that moment on, things took what I thought was a devastating turn in the wrong direction. I was sent home with orders to be on complete bed rest. No School. No church. Nothing, but attending doctor's appointments was expected of me. How would I graduate? This definitely is not what I envisioned for myself. Thankfully though, all, but one of my teachers allowed my work to be sent home for the last few weeks of my junior year. In addition to this, one of my most favorite educators on the planet brought me my finals and sat with me while I completed them. Because of her kindness I was able to keep my GPA up and graduate on time the next year ahead of my class. However, I opted out of the honors diploma to avoid such a rigorous load with a newborn. My main goal was to succeed and keep moving forward.

Halfway through my senior year of high school my brother and I got into a really nasty spat because I wouldn't allow him to use my cell phone. He became violent as he often did, and ended up grabbing me and throwing me onto the bed where my son was lying. I was shook up and called the police. They came and told him to leave until my mother arrived home. I was 18 at this point and was thinking I MUST go. Once my mother arrived home from work she let him back in. I told her since she did that I'd have to leave. She then took my car keys to a car that was in my name and paid for with my money. Then she sent me in her car to pick my sister up from work. I did it without protest. When I arrived home she knew I wouldn't leave that late. I took my keys and went to my room and began packing up all of our things and everything that I could fit into my Ford Contour. On the way to school the next morning, I called my cousin. She and her husband were like a second set of parents to me and I asked them if I could come and stay with them for a few days. I ended up staying with them until I started college the next fall.

So much happened in such a short time frame, including me leaving my son's father to escape the emotional abuse. I had no idea I was in a fight for my emotional stability. This realization came much later. It took a failed marriage, a new marriage and the arrival of my third child for me to have an ah-ha moment about motherhood and my upbringing.

In the above-mentioned situations, I was growing instinctively beyond myself to protect my children, but I had also carried some bad habits from my upbringing along with me; those subtle ones that you don't see as damning. Some of them were even cultural and something most Black people just do for extremely complex reasons.

While carrying my third little human, I realized that that was exactly what she was: a little human, to be perfectly whole upon her birth. I wasn't chosen to parent her or my older two children to change who God made them to be. I wasn't chosen to mold them into what I thought an ideal child should be. I WAS chosen to guide them into who they were divinely created to become. The truth is that this happens one way or the other whether parents help or hinder the process. I realized that the way a child is guided could seriously derail them in life. We are to share parts of ourselves with them so that they can glean from our experiences and prayerfully learn from our mistakes and take the path that their spirit leads them.

This was going to stretch me because it led me on a path in which I had to get closer to God. It helped me understand all the more who I was, and who I am. In turn it made me listen to whom my children were and are becoming. It's a frustrating thing when your children are strong-willed and give you much push back. I was raised that children should shut up and do what they're told. I wasn't very good at abiding by this rule growing up and neither are my smallest children, but for a long time I still pushed that on them.

There was something magical though that happened when I began my breastfeeding journey with my third child. I'd never been successful before, but I'd matured and had great support this time. I saw how easy it was for me to anticipate and meet her needs. And when I did we were connected in such a magnificent way that I understood when she was hungry, sleepy, or wet. The exchange that came when she was at the breast, the connection, and the satisfaction made me think of my connection to God. It works just the same. This new revelation cast a light and guided me to really get still and listen to all of my children and guide them in a way that was suitable to who they were.

It would be easy for me to parent my children all the same in a very stiff and rigid way, but what would I miss doing this?

It is a pain every time I have to concede and let them make a choice for themselves that I wouldn't make or that isn't necessarily convenient for me. But it is priceless watching how much they grow, self-examine, and gain self-confidence by taking part in making choices for themselves that they feel at the time are what they need to continue on in their own development. This certainly isn't a parenting model I had ever seen modeled in front of me. I really do drop the ball some days, but I will continue to grow past myself for the life of my children.

**Joi Barnett**

A Path to Queendom

As I look back and realize how far I have come, I realize all of the experiences that made me the woman I am today have been bittersweet. At the age of 40, I see images of each and every experience from the time I was 8 years old. I should be quite bitter, but my choice is to be grateful. Going through the struggle has gifted me many lessons learned and has informed my path to which I am seeking to continue to rise to my greatness.

It was about 3:00 am, when I heard shouting from the room diagonally across from mine. All I could hear was muffled crying and screams, "Stop!" The rumbling back and forth up and down the hallway was loud. I got out of bed and crawled on the floor to crack my door so I could see what was happening. There she was, my mother was crying for my big brother to stop, he had my father choked up against the wall, both of their eyes filled with rage and anger. I was so scared, but a bit of happiness filled me inside, because there was someone finally there to protect us; my brother, my rock, the one who cared for me and nurtured me. My brother finally saw my father hurting my mom and he came to rescue us. I came out of the room and stood in the hallway to watch. My bike went flying as they tussled back and forth, trying to prove who was stronger and mightier. Who was going to be the one left standing? It continued for some time and my brother yelled for me to go back to my room. I half-way did what I was told, instead of standing in the hallway, I stood with my door cracked opened. There was not much room, living in the projects, there wasn't much space to move around comfortably with everyone in the tiny little hallway. My mom disappeared for what seemed a long time. When she came back, there were two policemen with her.

Everything became confusing after that. My brother begged my mom to tell the police what was happening to us. He was 16 years old and that was the first time I saw my brother cry. My mother stood there and said nothing. She allowed my father to do the talking and he painted my brother as this angry little boy who attacked him. The court forbid my brother to return back to the house. My father won that night and he must of felt invincible but all I remember from that point is tears and sadness in the place I refused to call home. There were plenty of nights of muffled cries, days when my father would be home all day smoking crack and heroin with his friends. My mother worked 3 jobs to stay out of the home. I often stayed in my room alone and passed the time away with my imagination.

This lasted for a little while and I remember my brother coming to get my brother, my sister and I to bring us to stay at his girlfriend's house. They seemed to be more functional than my parents. This house was where I felt taken care of the most. They clothed us, fed us good food, took us to the movies and made us feel nurtured. Little did I know, my mom was trying to leave my father. During those years I landed in the hospital a lot. My last memory of my father was of me being home from school really sick. I remember lying in the bed next to him for a moment trying to catch my breath, coughing uncontrollably because I couldn't breathe. I was so afraid that if I closed my eyes once I was going to be dead. I couldn't understand why this man wouldn't call the ambulance. Soon my mother came in silent but furious and I honestly thought it was my fault and that she was upset with me. My mom clothed me, and we walked out of the door.

I remember my mother dragging me up the street, she seemed to be walking fast and I cried because now I thought, why on earth am I walking when I cannot breathe? I remember becoming dizzy and falling to the ground. Moments later, someone picked me up and put me in a brown station wagon. When I woke up I was in the ER with an IV and an oxygen mask over my face. Once my vision was focused I could see my mom. Her eyes looked bloodshot red. She had tissue fragments all over her face. I didn't dare ask her what was wrong... Who was that man that picked us up, because I knew she wouldn't tell me, that I would just have to wait and see how this all played out. The doctors came back to inform my mom that I would need to be admitted to the hospital and that I would need to be there for a few days because I had pneumonia. Hearing this was a sign of relief; the nurse's cared for me and were like family because I was in the hospital so often. There I knew I would be fed, get the caring and nurturing I needed and time away from such a dysfunctional place that lacked real love.

Within those cold white walls, my plan was to never to be like my parents. I would love, care and nurture my children no matter what. My home would be full of love, laughter, and bonding with my children. At a very young age I devoted my life to my children who were not even conceived yet. At some point my mom went and got a restraining order against my father and he had to leave the house. My brother came back and he worked to help my mom take care of us. After my father left, things seemed to calm down and things were a lot steadier. It finally functioned like a real home. I remember laughing more, and having friends come over to stay the night. I remember my mom smiling more and my brother making sure we were taken care of. As time went on, things started to shift and a new man came into the picture. Some of the same behaviors my mom allowed with my father surfaced and she was allowing them with them this new man. The only thing that was different was he wasn't beating her. He had other challenges, but we wouldn't discover that until years down the line.

The many things I saw as a child clouded my vision and my judgment. Subconsciously, I chose to be with a man that mentally, emotionally and physically abused me. In many ways, I chose someone who mirrored my father and thought he could love me like my father never did. I chose to be my mother, and deal with 16 years of abuse, and to behave in ways my mother behaved because that's all I knew. My children had suffered enough; my son was six years old the first time he saw his father lay his hands on me, and he was filled with so much anger and rage. My daughter was four years old when she first witnessed the abuse, and she too was filled with anger and rage. Both of my children reacted in different ways. One withdrew and went within, and the other was outwardly affected. After the birth of my third child things seemed to slip back to the old habits and the abuse began again. But this time, I couldn't allow another one of my babies to be affected.

In my heart I knew I was stronger than the path that was chosen for me. One night, after being beaten and then thrown in the shower to soothe my throbbing wounds, I made up in my mind that I would change my history, and history would stop repeating with me for the sake of my children. As I stepped out of the shower, he dabbed my wounds with a towel. I stared at myself in the mirror while going blank and hearing him say how he was sorry that he hurt me so badly. As I stared in that mirror, there was a girl I was sad for, a girl I knew was so tired, and who had become full of a silent rage. This girl looked back at me and whispered to my soul, "This is the very last time he will put his hands on you."

I became the woman who was leaving this man who was my husband, even if it killed me. That night in front of that mirror I decided to be who I was, and who my mother couldn't be.

The one caveat to this whole thing is that both of my children, one 23 years old and the other 21 years old are not repeating history and they are both in healthy relationships. They were both conscious about choosing mates that were supportive, loving, caring and nurturing. I Thank God for this!

Today, as I continue to heal from each experience and forgive all who hurt me knowingly and unknowingly, I strive to rise above it and turn my pain into something that will help others to forgive, heal and grow from their experiences, even if it hurts in the process. It has taken me some time to get here, but having these experiences has made me the Queen I am today.

 **Queen Shameka Charley**

Blissfully Falling into Oblivion and Existing without Reciprocity: Motherhood Was My Saving Grace

A traumatizing soul-death occurred, and it was a new chapter in my life. I fought daily to not let that dark experience overtake my soul and consume the power of my spirit or steal my light, but for nearly a year and a half, to no avail. I was drowning and I didn't have many I could genuinely look to for help. I felt completely empty inside, and having the slight baby blues didn't improve the situation although I later learned I was suffering from a hormonal imbalance and situational post-partum depression as a grieved the loss of a love that only superficially existed...

I am the culmination of a union that was purely sexual to say the least. A product of long nights, acts of adultery, the abuse of crack cocaine, and a mother's desire to have a beautiful Black child she hoped would gain her access into the loving Black family unit and present a love of her own to ease the desires of her lonely heart. Unfortunately, although my mother loved me something fierce and with every inch of her tattered soul, she struggled terribly with a spiritual hold in the form of an addiction to crack. Just like my father, she sought after crack to numb the pain she endured throughout her own childhood. She also fought desperately to escape the harsh reality of being on the receiving end of many conflicting types of love. Love that often fell short of what she yearned for endlessly throughout her life.

The contributor of my other DNA, my father, nearly 20 years my mother's senior, was a married man who stepped out on his Black wife who had bore him two sons before I was conceived. In addition to his crack addiction, he was silently fighting a battle with *bipolarism* and PTSD after being discharged from the army and neglected by the nation he had once served so proudly and bravely. Another Black man suffering silently...

In all of their brokenness and pain, these two united to create me. They brought forth new life, but little did they know, their pain, disappointment, love, joy, anguish and much more would be etched firmly into the very fabric of my DNA. Etched so deeply into the very the makeup of a portion of my soul that would remain untouched for years to come until I fell in love and dug deeply into my past pain and trauma to uncover it. For many years, I suppressed feelings that had been unconsciously passed along to me in my mother's womb, feelings that haunted me at the core of my being since the day the doctors violently cut me out of that safe haven that was my mother's belly.

"Now, everything I'm not... made me everything I am/Damn, here we go again," Kanye West said.

While I speak candidly about my disjointed conception and less than desirable beginning, the reality is that it hurts to know that I was a crack baby born of two people overcome by addiction and an innate heartache that festered away at their soul's for decades before I was even conceived. For many years this fact alone encouraged my heart to grow numb and it created a space that harvested strong feelings of abandonment, disappointment and prompted me to ask, why? While I'm forever grateful to my mother and father for doing the honorable thing and allowing my paternal grandparents to adopt me when I was 5 years old, sadly, this was my first experience with pain and heartache. I would not be able to articulate that pain or pinpoint its source or identify my deep desire to be loved and cared for by my own biological parents until I became a mother myself and experienced the most traumatic break up of my life...

Growing up with my grandparents on Detroit's west side, I was grieving the maternal and paternal sacred bonds my grandparents could never provide. Was I not good enough for my mother to get clean and give up the street life, drugs and prostitution? Was I not precious enough to encourage my father to admit I was his child and be a part of my life from the start? These were questions that lingered within every morsel of my being since childhood and have eaten away at my core, conscious, and subconscious for many years. Little did I know my dysfunctional beginning would provide the foundation for a heart that simply longed for a place to thrive; to be safe and to be protected while receiving reciprocal love that stretched far beyond both distance and time. I, in many ways, yearned and strived vigilantly to love hard because I thought if I loved hard enough the next person would not leave me the way those before them had. After all, this seems logical, right? But, I inherited my mother's enormous compassionate and giving heart, and my father's hunger for truth and knowledge and devout love for Black people and Black Power.

In March 2000, at the tender age of 11 years old another piece of my pulsating heart was violently ripped from my blossoming pubescent chest with no remorse, and my life would never be the same. My brother Rene Ali was murdered a few blocks from our home in broad daylight alongside a church located on one of the busiest residential streets in Detroit. Rene was not only my big brother, he was my best friend, my father figure, the one who proudly and wholeheartedly accepted me as his sister and publicly contested any notions that I was not *our* father's child regardless of how I was conceived.

After Rene was murdered, again I asked and sometimes even screamed at God, why? God clearly didn't understand that I needed Rene to protect me from the cold streets of Detroit! I was numb again and pissed at God because these situations continued to etch chapters of pain, sadness, and neglect unto my fragmented and already fragile young heart whether I realized what was happening or not! Was I not faithful enough to deserve my brother, my first champion? Was I not worthy of a consistent love of my own?

As a result of these two life experiences at a very young age I devised an escape plan from the hood plagued with violence, a place that proudly bred insecurities and heartbreak. I vowed to have a household free of drugs, free of hurt, free of painful family secrets, and abusers lurking in the dark hallways of our home. I vowed to create an unbreakable family bond with a beautiful Black man who was my equal! That was easier said than done because I truly did not know what that meant because I had very little models of what that looked like growing up. When I met Mya's father, I was taken aback by how much his demeanor, his "family first" mentality and his unyielding determination to overcome the adversity of the hood resembled the essence of my late brother Rene; I was drawn to him for these reasons. However, the moment I met him I sensed his own pain and brokenness. When I looked at him I could see pain in the depths of his tiny eyes and the deepness of his unspoken words. Little did I know bearing the burden of his trauma and pain would be the source of more heartache and pain than my family had ever dished out; it would deplete my soul of everything I had fought so hard to possess. Nearly two short years later I bore his seed and she was the most beautiful surprise, but she was conceived under toxic and hostile circumstances absent of the love I sought after all these years. I quickly learned I could not do his heavy lifting and sifting through his trauma; it literally sucked the life out of me.

"When you submit your will to someone a piece of you dies."

Her father and I knew we were both dying inside. We were wearing masks and were unable to be true to ourselves, but still we welcomed our baby girl with the most loving and generous open hearts because she was our hope that true unconditional love did exist. Her love was untainted and free from hurt... unlike our own. The harsh reality was that Mya represented a love unlike anything we'd ever experienced; pure, unconditional, and innocent, without heartbreak... A love of our own that we could nurture! Her love made me think about Lauryn Hill's song, Zion...and these words spoke to me:
"Unsure of what the balance held/I touched my belly overwhelmed/By what I had been chosen to perform/But then an angel came one day/Told me to kneel down and pray/For unto me a [wombman] child would be born/Woe this crazy circumstance/I knew [her] life deserved a chance/But everybody told me to be smart/Look at your career they said/Jasmine, baby use your head/But instead I chose to use my heart."

I would ultimately feel the love I'd waited for, in fact it gestated in my womb for exactly 39 weeks and 4 days! She would become the only soul who knew the sound of my heartbeat, who heard my cries of loneliness late at night, a soul that would ease the excruciating pain I had unconsciously suppressed for so long.

To her father, I was simply a disposable vessel who would birth the only soul worthy of his unconditional love. Sadly, after the birth of our baby girl my worth rapidly deteriorated and I was holding on desperately to a man who refused to fight to love me because he secretly despised everything I stood for.

Day in and day out, I walked around with my heart beating outside of my chest. I was bleeding profusely while racking my brain to find solutions to the madness of his cold heart, but to no avail. I cried secretly for months in isolation. I would drop Mya off at school and drive to work and cry in my car in the parking garage, then gather my face, fix my crown and walk into my office and play the part like nothing happened. Inside I was broken and numb because this was not the way I envisioned motherhood or the structure of my own little family. To say the least, I was a functionally depressed person who also suffered from anxiety because I was experiencing gas lighting at home. It seemed like the more I attempted to mend our little family, the less respect he had for me as a woman and a mother, because to him I represented weakness and was unlike the women in his family because I showed vulnerability. Frankly, I was striving to love a heart that was guarded with a bulletproof vest.

Eventually, I developed anxiety due to constantly overthinking and analyzing things, which quickly turned into postpartum depression. For months I suffered in silence and I did not utter those words, not even to my own mother or my closest friends. I was too embarrassed of being seen as weak in their eyes, because according to them I had been *"so strong for years"* and *"this is no different"*. After all, I was a strong Black *wombman* with an

"S" etched on my chest, and I was going to be a damn good mother no matter what the circumstances were. Many refer to this as the "strong Black woman superhero complex."

The moment when everything changed was when I looked into the eyes of my 8-month-old infant as she wiped my tears with a sad and confused look on her face. She could feel my pain and that broke me down even more! It was then that I knew I had to walk away and let go of this soul tie that no longer served me.

And, after nearly two years of arguing and having conflicts over almost everything, verbal and emotional abuse and realizing he could only give me the dysfunctional love he had, I finally chose me. I gathered all of my shit left and it was one of the hardest things I've ever had to do. Although I was terrified to leave because I feared I would harm my child in the process whether it be physically or emotionally or both, I walked out the door and didn't look back. A rebirth was in order, and I fully embraced the journey. I was preparing myself to rise like a Phoenix, a bird that has lived many generations and still soared, I was regenerated and ready to fly through the burnt ashes, but the road to recovery was far from easy.

After this traumatizing bout I was exhausted and distraught and couldn't even recognize myself anymore. I had forgotten how to be that carefree person. I even questioned my intelligence and my beauty and my confidence, something I hadn't done my entire life. Although it was excruciating and extremely arduous, I began the long journey of restoration, healing, rebranding and connecting with pieces of myself I'd lost, and discovering new pieces of myself along the way. They say, "You never know how strong you are until strength is the only option and your back is against a wall."

For nearly a year, I secretly struggled with post-partum and it wasn't until I saw a therapist did I even accept and acknowledge that's what I had experienced. During my postpartum bouts, which are less frequent now, I find myself struggling to get out of bed, eat or simply clean my place because I feel as if I have given everything I have to the world, to my child, and to my community with little in return. Who nurtures the mama when she needs to be rejuvenated? Although I am a strong wombman, many days I feel alone in this journey and wonder when I've cared for everyone and given my all away who is going to take care of me?

Mya is my rainbow and each day I feel like I don't deserve her, but I know she is my blissful balance of joy and pain. After 25 hours of natural labor and birth like a true warrior Goddess, Mya gracefully joined us earth side and she was the most precious being I'd ever laid eyes on! Only moments after her birth, I noticed something unique about this lovely soul that had gestated in my womb and listened to my heartbeat. We shared the same unique heart-shaped birthmark on our stomachs. The only difference is hers was located on the left side of her stomach and mine is located on the right side. This alone was confirmation that she had been handpicked to accompany and guide me through motherhood and life; I needed her more than she needed me.

I was forced to unlearn the cycle of dysfunctional love that plagued so many homes in the Black community. In order to accomplish this feat, I have committed to showing my daughter what true unconditional love looks and feels like. Many days I fall short, and I question my ability to be responsible for such a precious being, but my heart is pure and I have learned how to love her through much trial and error. *Tupac said it best, "Because this is my rose and these are my damaged petals.*" Seen in this way, I am not perfect and I am a work in process but the reality is I'm continuing to work and unlearn the harmful ways of my upbringing and my child is teaching me so much in the process.

I have purely welcomed Mya into this world and into my life, and I have accepted the *privilege* of being her mother first and foremost. I have vowed to do better than my parents and together we will break the generational curses placed on her father and I. She is my baby girl and on my lowest days I live vicariously through her. But to say that motherhood is extremely difficult is an understatement, it is the absolute toughest position I've ever had. Each day Mya gives me life, especially when living is the last thing I want to do. As her mother, I endure the weight of the world to protect her from chaos, and I continue to transform the pain birthed by that chaos into pure love and joy even through all the pain I have suffered in silence.

Conscious and compassionate parenting is like putting a mirror up to yourself and looking deeply into your own soul to see your imperfections. I wholeheartedly believe, how we treat our children is subconsciously a direct reflection of how we see and treat ourselves.

Pregnancy and birth is a divine process by which the child passes through the womb that serves as the spiritual gateway between the spirit and the physical worlds. Because we are magnificently and wonderfully made, The Creator designed the womb to take on the DNA of our children during this process. Not only do we take on their DNA, which remains, in our wombs, they take on ours and carry our past traumas with them. We are forever changed. Seen in this way, our children are a reflection and an image of us as well as all of those ancestors who have come before us! When I find myself mothering in a way that I'm ashamed of, I have to dig deep in the crevices of my soul and do some restoration and healing of self because I know that I am unconsciously mothering my daughter in a way that imitates my feelings toward myself. She is because I am...

Motherhood is spiritual work and when you need spiritual work and to build a relationship with yourself you notice it through the relationship you have with your children and others. Do you see them? Do you feel them? Are you compassionate? Pain and suffering that is not worked through and given the proper attention will create an environment where your self-hatred will unconsciously fester and that unfelt pain will be passed on to your children and loved ones. Unfortunately, I had to learn this harsh lesson the hard way.

What motherhood has also taught me is that I am mothering from a place of absence. I spent most of my childhood "motherless" because my mother was living her life and searching for herself in some very lonely places in the streets. As a result of that, when I found out I was with child, I rationalized that I would always be attached to my child and have an established emotional bond with her no matter what and how hard the process would be. Sadly, at times, I over compensate for my mother's absence through my own mothering. Although my mother and I have a great relationship now and I'm grateful she returned to me clean and with an open heart. There are parts of me that my mother may not ever understand as a result of her missing the crucial first years of my life.

I had no idea what "attachment parenting was" although I saw countless pictures of my siStars baby wearing and completing daily tasks with babies wrapped firmly on their backs or suckling dreamily at their breasts, however, I knew it was something I yearned for my daughter and myself to establish that maternal sacred bond. In many ways, the mothering of my daughter is nurturing my younger self that was neglected and forced to grow numb far too early due to the circumstances of my upbringing. Sadly, I didn't really have any consistent person to attach to.

Many people in the village know me as "that breastfeeding wombman," but I haven't uttered to a soul that one of the many reasons I choose to nurse my child aside from the historical context of Black wombmen being forced to wet-nurse the oppressors children, was that I'm a crack baby and my mom said she was afraid her "milk was no good for me because of the drugs." Just typing those words, made my soul cringe and I could hear the shame in my mother's voice when she shared those words with me when I asked her why she hadn't given me her breast milk. My mother had shared with me before that she was using drugs before she found out she was pregnant but I didn't make the connection that her milk was "spoiled." As a result of this, I fight battles daily, within myself and the world, to give my child, and to support other women to give their children the very best we have to offer, straight from our Goddess frames.

My chocolate milk is revolutionary and not only does it create a solid healthy foundation, I know that I am giving her an emotional attachment and stability in a mother figure that I craved as a child. Breastfeeding has been very taxing, emotionally, physically and even mentally because I'm in warrior stance day in and day out standing for my child's human rights and my right to take back ownership of my Black female body. When I nurse her, I show the world and myself that my child matters, I matter and my womb matters because it is no longer property of this racist nation. This is the most powerful thing I've done in my whole life and to say it is the hardest is a massive understatement as well... But fists up, breasts out... the revolution starts with motherhood and without wombmen, there is no revolution. Mothering is revolutionary and challenging harmful mindsets is revolutionary too!

Each day is another day to get in the ring and fight viciously against the perils of life that haunt me and set out to defeat me... but I'm made for this beautiful struggle and there is no other option but to prevail; the truth is I'm just asking to have my humanity restored in the process and not be seen as a victim but as a survivor because one day my daughter will be someone's mother and I don't want her to been seen as not human as she faces the violent blows life throws her way as a Black wombman. I am strong, but many refuse to see that strength comes in many forms and sometimes it's the ability to admit when I'm weak or hurting or need help that is the true display of my strength. The truth is that breaking is not an option for Black mothers and I have a beautiful Black princess attentively watching every move I make so I have to fight for space for Black wombmen to heal and be surrounded by their village. Mya is my revolution and I have to be around to see her grow and blossom and to pass on the knowledge that she is never alone. Black motherhood is revolutionary and I'm learning to do it differently with her so that the cycle does not repeat itself. I'll bend, but I'll never break... Ashé.

 *Jasmine Tane't Boudah*

Untitled

I am a mother.
I am not perfect.
I am flawed.
I make mistakes.
I love.
I love hard.
I teach.

Sometimes I forget to be gentle.
Sometimes the pressures of life cause me to ignore my children a little longer than I want to.
Sometimes I scream.
Sometimes I am impatient.
Sometimes I go to bed thinking I have failed them.
Sometimes I go to bed feeling like the best mother in the world.

I am hard on myself.
So I vent.
Sometimes I vent to people who don't understand.
I expect support.
I get judgment.
I feel worse as a mother.

Sometimes my children glow when they see me.
Sometimes I feel they are tired of me and can't stand me.

Sometimes I grow tired of them.
Sometimes I glow when I see them.
Sometimes I don't teach.
Sometimes they learn anyhow.
Sometimes they have too much screen time.
Sometimes there isn't enough of me to go around.

Sometimes one gets ignored more than the other.
Sometimes their meals aren't as nutritious as I'd like.
Sometimes I make mistakes.
Sometimes I don't.
Sometimes I think I'm raising brilliant children.
Sometimes I think I'm effing them up for life.
Sometimes they are uber cute.
Sometimes they stink.
Sometimes I cry.
Sometimes I smile.

All the time I am a mother.
All the time I am not perfect.
All the time my love is perfect.
All the time they are resilient.
All the time my intentions are pure.

I am a mother.
I am flawed.
But my love is not.

 **Sona Smith**

Untitled

Five years ago today on January 8th, I came home from the hospital with my first-born Ayah Sol. Sent home on *day 3*, to heal physically from major abdominal surgery and spiritually and emotionally from having everything I knew to be true about my body's ability to birth my baby without intervention chewed up, swallowed and spit back out in my face by a medical system that didn't care that I was well-read, well-prepared, and well-supported. All they cared about was that a monitor told them my baby's heart rate wasn't strong enough to endure the strength of my contractions after having been in labor so long and still only being at 3cm dilated.

They didn't care that my midwife and the nurses all supported me laboring longer. They didn't care that I was contracting every two minutes with no pain relief as they tried to talk to me in medical jargon I completely understood but was in no space to debate. They scoffed at the fact the Elisha knew everything I knew, and they weren't prepared for this educated, strong, Black man to advocate for his child and me... in their language. They didn't care that the most beautiful day of our lives became the scariest, and that our desire to get our baby here safely trumped everything even without their scare tactics, fear mongering, and trickery.

They didn't realize that even a slight shift in their tone would've made signing the paperwork and submitting to having my uterus cut wide open and my baby pulled from a scar would've made all the difference in my mental and emotional well-being. They didn't realize I had already dreamt my child was born while I was sleeping, not once, but three times throughout my pregnancy--- when they failed to inform me before signing that paper because I had not had an epidural prior to that. There was no time for a spinal and I would have to be put under. They didn't realize I respected birth enough to know that sometimes shit happens, and in the case we needed a C-section I was okay as long as I had my strength by my side.

Sadly, they nonchalantly ripped Elisha away from me without notice when they kept rolling my bed into the operating room and they made him stop at the OR doors because he couldn't be present while I was being put under. They didn't prepare me to not say goodbye. And that mean ass doctor didn't realize that her taking a message to him while I was being shaved, strapped down, lights in my face, hearing the buzzing of residents, nurses, and doctors as they speculated why Ayah's heart rate was going so slow meant the world to me, but I forgave her anyway. They didn't care that the Caribbean nurse who tried every natural way possible to raise Ayah's heart rate dropped a few tears as she told me to take a deep breath and count down from 10. I don't remember anything past 5, but I remember that same nurse holding my hand when I woke up.

They didn't care that I wasn't the first to hold my precious baby or that I wanted to strip her down to nothing because by the time she got to me she was bathed and fully clothed. I wanted to study every inch of her body. But the meds made me shake and shiver uncontrollably and I couldn't even hold my dear baby to my breast without Elisha's help. I couldn't change her diaper; I couldn't sit up or get her to latch because the scar on my womb hurt me to the core. They didn't know how disheartening it was to have to fight to breastfeed because they just assumed I was going to be a formula-feeding mom as a result of my marital status and skin color. The shock on their faces every time they walked in the room for entire 3 days we were there asking why Elisha hadn't left was priceless. He never left my side and they couldn't handle that, not from a Black man and his family. They didn't know that though I was happy to have my baby here with me, I was traumatized to the point of nightmares and flashbacks for years after giving birth. And that even as I type this I cry from the pain, not just because they cut my uterus but because they tried to slash my spirit in the process.

I went home bent but not broken, and I continued to process it all. I asked Elisha over and over again what we could've done differently. Before I knew it, postpartum depression overtook me in ways I never imagined. I loved my baby, but I was so sad. No one understood that, so I kept my tears to myself and suffered silently. I sought support groups but no one in the circle looked like me, so again I cried alone and suffered in silence. Where was a Black mother to go to discuss her ails and struggles with motherhood and postpartum depression? I soon found my voice, and my passion to be a doula was born, naturally, without epidural, and no C-section was needed. My desire to be an advocate, a supporter, and a fighter of women's rights was stronger than them and the system that gave birth to them effortlessly. So here I am. I didn't need them to affirm me when I had two VBACs after that C-section, which is completely against the controlling nature of Western medicine. I didn't VBAC to prove to them that I could, I did it for Ayah. She was there; right there when Moonbeam was born because SHE deserved to experience birth as our Creator intended it.

My body wasn't broken; her heart wasn't weak. I don't regret it, because I don't think I would've had to reach into the depths of my soul to discover the magic of my womb if not for this traumatic birthing experience.

The universe is funny that way, I was prepared through my prenatal dreams. My birth classes beforehand were confirmation for me that I did what I needed to do to get my Sol here and not an ounce of me feels as if I failed. I gave birth, to Ayah Sol on that day and I gave birth to myself as well... We came home on 1/10/10 ready for life ready for love...

We went home on Day 3, resurrected and risen...

 **Sona Smith**

What the Blogs Don't Tell You

It was actually three months after my uncle lost his battle with H.I.V and alcoholism that I found out I was pregnant. I was terrified… my husband of eight months at the time and I had been trying after five months of being married, in attempt to give my mother a chance to meet her grandchild. She was battling cancer for two years and while she fought every day, she was becoming less and less of herself as time passed. Unfortunately, she passed away before I could grant that wish for her. It's like as soon as I found out I was pregnant I instantly worried every single day. What kind of mother would I be? How was I supposed to raise a child in this cold world? Who would he or she look like? These questions were swirling in my mind.

See, I wanted him chocolate just like my mom, but I also prayed it wasn't my uncle's soul reborn, since reincarnation is something I strongly believe in. You see I loved my uncle to death but I wouldn't know how to deal with a spirit like his! My uncle was so fiery and independent; a man in his own sense. A man who knew his mistakes, and knew he made a lot of them but still stood on his own two feet. Did I want my son to be like that? Black men haven't had the best track record at this point, not that it's ever been easy being a Black man in America but imagine being one with heart who took no bullshit. Makes you a walking target just for having an opinion. Was I even pregnant with a boy? It'll be easier with a girl, right?

Black women have it a bit easier here, right? However, because of social networking, a new light has been shed on our country, things that would often go unheard of would be national news and even if you weren't trying to follow certain stories one couldn't help but cringe when you realize how cruel people could be to those occupying a Black body. In many ways, finding out that I was pregnant was both the happiest moments and the beginning of one of the most worrisome phases of my life. I wanted to make the best decisions for my child with hopes of the most fulfilling future possible.

Though I had a pretty routine pregnancy with minimal stress, was healthy and not over worked, I still gave birth to my son 5 weeks early weighing 4lb 13 oz. He stayed in the NCIU at Fairbanks Memorial Hospital 10 days excruciating before he was approved to go home. He was delivered 13 hours after I noticed I was leaking fluids while sleeping. The original hospital wasn't equipped to have preemies so I was transferred to the local hospital where I received exceptional care. I was able to have my child naturally with my labor and in water, ate, and felt like I was actually listened to and considered throughout the laboring and birthing process. I was visited by lactation consultants before and after labor and was given a ton of breastfeeding tips and equipment to prepare for my breastfeeding journey. When I decided to breastfeed it had been simply because it was the best decision to me, for my child. There are so many types of formulas, and I just think he'd never get the right amount of nutrients.

When I thought about how powerful my body was gestating and giving birth naturally, I also knew it would get the job done and be equipped to nourish him. It was difficult initially because my son wouldn't latch on which forced me to use nipple shields and syringes to help the process. Some days I couldn't produce enough milk, which pushed me to give him donated milk. It makes you feel less of a person just thinking that you don't have what it takes to just do it on your own and provide everything your child needs. What you don't learn from blogs is that the most natural things are the most demanding and complicated!

All of the talks with lactation consultants and nurses didn't help soothe my overworking mind. I just wanted to do what was best for my son, all I wanted was to get it together for him. Other than the feedings every two hours, I'd say it was almost like being on a nice vacation in the hospital. I was even given a room to stay in once I was discharged from the hospital so I could visit my son whenever I wanted. Although I hated the fact that he came early, I was very appreciative of all the support and care I received because it helped me set a strong foundation for when I got home and had to care for him without nursing staff.

To say the least, it's been an experience, some days I vow never to have any more children, other days I'm convinced one more will be perfect for my husband and our beautiful family. Being in Alaska isolated from friends and family puts a lot of the load on me with my husband being an active military member who works over 12 hours most days. With no family around I don't have the comfort I need to leave him and go back to work, so I plan on being a stay-at-home mom for now.

Those ten days seemed to last forever and 26th of September release date couldn't have come any sooner. In time, I was producing more milk, and then one random day I placed him on my nipple to feed and he latched on and we've been doing it that way ever since. He's in the weight group he'd be in if he was born on time, he's laughing, baby babbling, reaching, and noticing things and people. I'm so proud of him! We've come a long way.

Being a mom has come with a lot of worry and sleepless nights. I've only been a mother for 15 weeks at this point and he's changed me so much already. Breastfeeding hasn't been easy and keeping up with Jackson, my son, has been very demanding and exhausting at times but it's become so natural now. I don't even wake up fully to nurse him, I'll just lay him on my chest use the "lazy latching position" and he finds the milk himself, it's so adorable and even miraculous! In the time we've been together we've created a bond so strong, and I can't wait to see how it flourishes over the course of his life. He will always be my number one priority. I will always make the best decision I have available for him, no matter how difficult or demanding it may be for me. He will grow to be a strong, respectable, and intelligent Black man.

 *Jhayla Carter*

When Love Is Not Enough

For the third time in ten years, we tried to be together again and after weeks of me trying to make it work, despite his yelling through defensive lies we ended things for good. He wanted nothing to do with me and I wanted nothing to do with this baby that *WE* chose to create *ON PURPOSE*. I hated that I was pregnant. I had hoped stress and anger would allow me to miscarry, because I was too afraid to get an abortion; although abortion was high on my list. All I could think was "*I don't want this baby*", "*I hope I lose this baby, "Why me?*"

On December 7, 2012 at my first appointment, I heard the heartbeat for the first time, but I still didn't want this baby. Moments later, I was sent to get an ultrasound to confirm I was as far along as I said I was. I saw that fetus; moving, kicking, and sucking its thumb. We laughed. That made the baby turn on its side as if it was trying to get some privacy. I pretended to enjoy this moment, but only for my five-year-old daughter's sake, because she was there to witness this as well. The tech sent us back to the Dr. so he could explain that the baby had an abnormality and was measuring smaller than expected. I was sent to a specialist days later, where the horrible news was confirmed; *my baby had a genetic disease and I was told I should terminate immediately because the prognosis was already fatal.* It felt like someone threw an ax into my chest. My heart began to tear deeply and slowly.

I felt sorry, ashamed, and I hated myself. I took every test I could take and they all confirmed the same; either my baby would die in the womb, or immediately following birth. Termination was now top on my list, but not to spare my baby's journey; it was to spare my *own* heart and the heart of my 5-year-old who was looking forward to becoming a big sister. I tried to find the $1,400 it would take to end this pregnancy, and eventually had a reliable source to provide it. But it was something my big girl said that changed my mind; she said, "*I would want to meet this baby if it were ME.*" That's when I knew I was obligated to endure this process, even though it would turn out to be the most depressing journey of my life.

I can't begin to tell you how hard this journey was. Everyone was so excited for this baby growing in me, and here I was not even wanting to know the gender of the fetus. But, my first born was so excited about being a big sister that she told the whole world and made friends everywhere we went. When I was four months pregnant I had a dream, in that dream my baby revealed to me that she was a girl. I was devastated. I had hoped it would be a boy, assuming that I wouldn't be as attached to it if it were.

Six months in, I still didn't want confirmation of the gender, because I felt it didn't matter; I didn't want this fetus anyway. But my loving 5-year-old felt differently. I told her, "*We're having a baby, but we may not be able to keep it because it is sick. Do you still want to know what it is?*" She said, "Yes". I asked, "*Do you still want to give it a name?*" She said, "Yes," I said. Six months into it, the specialist confirmed that the fetus was in fact a girl and that she did in fact have the genetic disease, Trisomy 18, which meant she wasn't going to make it. I cried. For months, for weeks, for days, for hours, for minutes, for seconds; I cried. I can't tell you how many times I rubbed that big ole belly telling her "*Mommy's SO sorry. I DO love You. I DO want You. I DO hope you make it.*" I blamed myself for her illness, regardless of what the genetic specialist told me. I just knew God was punishing me for not loving my baby enough. I had so many dreams of my future, and *this* baby wasn't in any of them, and that's when I knew I would not be able to keep her.

May 28, 2013, I had to be induced early because I was producing too much amniotic fluid that the baby wasn't ingesting, which was proof her brain wasn't developed enough to perform these natural functions due to this genetic disease. In comparison, my first experience with childbirth was so easy. No epidural, no pain and I had been in labor for 23 hours. But *this* time, only 9 hours of labor, and it was the most painful experience of my life. I told my best friend, "*If my baby doesn't come out crying, please don't let me go crazy.*" It was time to push, but I wasn't ready. I tried my best to keep her in my womb as long as I could because I wasn't ready to say goodbye. The nurses thought I was holding back to wait for the doctor, but I was attempting to stall because I wasn't ready to let her go. The pain became unbearable. Three pushes later, she came; she was born into complete silence. I don't think I've ever heard a room so quiet. No one said anything and nothing moved, it was as if time too had stood still. I had no energy to hold my baby, and no heart to look at her until minutes later, and my 5-year-old walked in skipping her way to the bed to show us the teddy bear she got for her baby sister from the hospital gift shop. They cleaned my sweet baby and we held her for as long as we could; passing her around between myself, her big sister, her Godmother, and my friend. The nurse was even a part of the rotation, but only to check her vitals, waiting to confirm her death.

Three hours later, on May 29th, my best friend started crying, and begged me to take my baby from her arms. I did. I held her and I gently stroked her chubby cheeks, I wrapped her tiny hands around my finger, and calmly watched her soul slip away from her quaint five pound body. She was perfect, fully developed, and nothing looked abnormal. Then she went. My big girl didn't understand what was wrong until her Godmother (my best friend) picked her up, and told her, *"The Baby is gone"*. She was initially lost, but figured it out soon enough and she cried until her tears drowned her with slumber. When it was time; and when I was ready, my baby was removed from my arms.

I held my big girl as she slept the rest of the night, until more tears woke her up from her sleep. I couldn't function by myself. All I could think was *how do I go on being a mother to the daughter I already have (the one I was allowed to keep), and properly mourn and punish myself for the daughter I didn't love enough, who became an angel instead?* I didn't want to see anyone; I didn't want to hear anyone. I didn't even want to exist. Every night I soaked my healing body in the bath tub, I cried until the water was too cold for me to sit in it. Then I'd run more hot water, lay there, and cry some more until I was too tired to cry at all. Then I'd lay in bed with my (almost 6-year-old) big girl and try to sleep. I went to bed with tears, and woke up with more tears in my attempts to have a normal day. It became routine: Wake up crying, brush my teeth, eat my egg whites, turkey bacon, and brown sugar & cinnamon oatmeal, and sit around watching reality T.V (because the drama was the only thing that could take me away from my own thoughts), soak my healing body while crying and then lay in bed until I cried myself to sleep, and then I'd do the exact same thing the next day.

A little time had passed by, and I thought I was handling things fairly well. Then one night I was taking my routine soaking, when my milk came in. I broke down in a way that I didn't think I could fix. Every drop was a reminder that I was producing milk for a baby that I gave birth to, but wasn't allowed to keep. Every contraction of my uterus was a reminder that I was healing from giving birth to a baby I wasn't allowed to keep. Every time I attempted to exercise, it was a reminder that I was trying to lose weight from giving birth to a baby that I wasn't allowed to keep. I would drive two cities over, just to run errands to avoid running into all the people who recognized me, and would have noticed my empty belly and ask all the questions I wasn't ready to answer. I started counseling, but only because it was a mandated portion of the physical I had to take before I could return to work. I expressed anger, sadness, regret, sadness, hate, sadness, resentment, and more sadness. I finally understood what it felt like for people who committed suicide. It's like you have this pain that is so unbearable that all you want is for it to stop, and ending your life seems to be the only way.

A year later, I was better and ready to face the world and its many questions. I could finally sing again, and the first song I wrote after a 2-year hiatus was of course, a song for **Her**. Two and a half years, countless tears, and five songs later, I can finally breathe again, but for some reason I can't say Her name. I only call her *"My Baby"*, unless people ask, *"What did you name Her?"* Just today, two people asked if my (now) 8-year-old is my only one, and I still pause when I answer the question. *My Angel Baby is worth talking about, worth acknowledging, and worth celebrating.* Even though God took Her back to be with Him, He knew what He was doing by giving me my big girl first. She celebrates and honors her baby sister in any and every way possible. I can't look at the color "purple" without smiling, for it's the color my big girl chose to honor her baby sister's memory.

I finally went back to work when God saw that I was ready, and He puts me in a classroom full of children that are my Angel Baby's age. One little girl was born May 29, 2013, a day after my Baby. Yeah, God's funny like that. It's still hard for me to pray. Sometimes I feel it's pointless because God is going to do what He wants to do anyway. Other times I pray just to say that I did, but only for others, not for myself. Every night I close my eyes hoping, that tonight's the night I dream about Her. As of December 28, 2015, I have yet to do so. But I cherish a dream I had during my maternity leave. I saw an angel I went to high school with, whom I had dreamt about a few times before. I asked him if he met my baby yet. He shook his head and said, "no". I told him, "*My baby will be coming there (Heaven) soon, and when she gets there please tell her I miss Her, and I'm sorry I didn't love Her enough.*" He said he would, so now I patiently wait for his message from Her.

Until Then,

 *Leslie Sain*

It Wasn't Enough

His words lacked love
The epitome of a broken heart
Seeking revenge
Not knowing where to start
The mere feeling of being disrespected
Was the path you chose

The pain, the hurt and the poison was already injected
Giving him the better half of me
Knowing the child wouldn't help him grow
My child, who yearned for my love and heartbeat
Was the beginning of my glow

Not one time, but twice
Did I indulge in a fool?
Thinking the essence of his seed
Would be his first day of school
The love was never there
Neither was the strive

But the one inside of me
Kept me alive
I yearned for the moment
To be loved and appreciated
But the youngin' inside of you
Could only produce hatred

This is not how I imagined things to be
The high, the low, the rough and the tough
Only to realize
The heartbeat nor the meeting was enough

 **Bianca L. Smith**

Untitled

After my daughter was born I got even bigger. I was up to a size 22 at the biggest and I am only 5'1". I was trying to work, bring my baby to work, living in an apartment and I wasn't getting along well with her father so we broke up and I moved in with my parents with my baby. It was at that moment I realized I was going to be a single mom with the support of my immediate family, my mom and dad.

I changed jobs, started working out, got a house in the neighborhood and moved on with life. I was dating, partying, being in shows, taking my daughter with me on teaching gigs and residencies. Going, going, and going all the time, which took my mind off anything I didn't want to think about. I was making art and interfacing with the professional dance world, academia, the public school system, philanthropic organizations and grant makers. I was sitting on boards of organizations and teaching at so many different venues. The main focus of my motherhood was on showing my daughter how to follow her dreams and to keep pushing even in the face of single motherhood.

I never realized how guilty I felt for being a single mom, for my daughter not having her father in her life. I also compensated a lot for what I wish I had when I was young; more freedom, more friends, more connections. Now that my daughter has those things I find myself not only resentful of her fresh new journey, but also sad about many things, about discipline she now lacks because I never wanted her to lack opportunity. I am so surprised constantly by the way motherhood changes as children grow into the people they always were.

My son and daughter are eight years apart with two different fathers and grew up very differently. Although I was married to his father, we split after only 4 years of living together. He left the state when his son was three years old and I know I overcompensated with love and experiences with my son. I have so much anger about single parenting that it's hard not to take it out on the children in some way - either too much hollering or spoiling them too much; both bring us out of balance. All of us are struggling with the depression of being abandoned. I think I am doing better with my son, or at least building upon the lessons I learned from parenting my daughter thus far. In retrospect, I now realize the importance of consistency and just being there, being still and available to catch the moments that can easily be missed with my children when life is moving so quickly. My son is also struggling with reading and paying attention in school. I'm working with him more on things that came naturally to my daughter. He's still young though, and thinks the world of me. My son is still homebound and connected to mom intimately. He doesn't see all my shortcomings or pick at my weak spots the way my daughter can. Now that she's getting older and more independent I realize I am panicking, and feelings of abandonment are looming in the shadows. I have to remember that she's not her dad, and she's always been meant to fly.

Another struggle is remembering not to blame anyone for someone else's behavior. No one is just like their dad or their sister or brother...and I am not just like my parents. There are so many chances to slip up and throw blame around, but I'm trying to focus on building healthy relationships with my children so they will talk to me. I found that fully enforcing my expectations feels like I'm being too oppressive in the moment. But, later on when I'm reflecting on my parenting I feel that I got my respect and made the lesson clear to my child. Spoiling, being lenient, impulsive and exasperated is a helpless mode of parenting that I slip into without realizing it. Once I get stuck in that low place it takes the reminder of certain grounding activities to try to pull our family back in sync. Things like drumming, dancing, working with music, arts, food, and culture, even just connecting with play or writing, drawing, making things, going to the library or the YMCA. Our family has a deep connection to Black arts and culture in many different ways in the community.

Like me, my children grew up saturated in positive and realistic reflections of Blackness and our African heritage. Even though I sent them to private schools in very white dominated spaces, I see them confident inside their Blackness. I see them accepting so many different angles of Blackness because of their own self-acceptance and intentional exposure. They are both conscious and involved in the struggle for Black liberation. Because we are grounded in Blackness and we talk openly about our present and past as Black Americans, we are so connected to our "Africaness" as well, considering my son's father is from West Africa. In many ways, I live an Afrocentric life that spills over into every aspect of motherhood. It goes very deep; releasing white ideas about who we are and who our children are as well.

Pregnancy was miserable for me both times, but taking care of a baby is nothing compared to the scope of what parenting has turned out to be. My babies have developed into people and there is a constant negotiation in providing guidance and structure to support them. Parenting is literally the most difficult task I will ever undertake. It's a lifelong job and position, but more than that, parenting requires a ton of mental energy, concentration, and creativity. The inherent personhood of my children has been a tough and beautiful lesson that I still work to master.

Anonymous Black Lotus Mother

Burning Bush

I did not fall in love with my son in utero or at first sight, not the first time he suckled on my breast or the first night we spent together, not with his first smile, or even his first step. For me, pregnancy, labor, birth, and motherhood weren't magical in the way in which I expected. There was no tingly feeling, no joy; at least not one that was familiar. I did not have post-partum. I was not unhappy. I was not sad. It was something else. It was a lack of something. Something I expected to be there, but wasn't.

I will disclaim that what I am describing wasn't a lack of love. I loved my son along the way; at every step really. I knew I loved my son. I sacrificed myself effortlessly for him every day. But, I also expected more happiness because of this child. And I didn't feel that. It always made me feel amiss.

Tingly feelings aside, what I was, and this much I knew, was different because of my son. As different, as foreign and unexplainable as the void of reasonable emotion one could feel towards their own child. My core was different. The voice inside my head was different. The tone in which I spoke to myself was different. There was a spiritual stillness within me as well as a fire. There was urgency. There was purpose. I thought differently. I felt differently. I was overwhelmed with the idea of service. There was an awakening inside of me, and with it a detachment from almost everything I was conditioned to know and love. The *magically romanticized mother-child bond* I expected in pregnancy and at so many moments during those first years never came. What did come instead was a welcomed soundness, a calm, a peace. *De ja vu of sorts*; it was a feeling I could not qualify but could identify as mine to have.

Somewhere around 18 months, my son's constant jumping up on me triggered unresolved emotions about sexual assault and abuse I had not dealt with. Because these emotions were surfacing as a result of my child's actions and because I lived with my child, I could not escape them, I was forced to live with my issues, and in turn, resolve them.

At the height of his absolute cuteness at around ages 2-3, I became aware of my relationship with praise and self-value, of production and self-worth. That process required me to take an in-depth look at the value I myself placed on how hard I worked in exchange for praise, acceptance, and love.

Between the ages of 4-5, my son hit a wall of emotional defiance, rage, and brokenness. He was tough. Tough to deal with. Tough to understand. Tough to manage. Impossible to control. This phase was more difficult than I could have ever predicted or prepared for. There was a lot of crying and screaming, manipulating, and even hitting. In a desperate attempt to not lose my mind I took to meditation and prayer. I read and I wrote in my journal. I cried a lot. I became conscious of my breath. Some days, I got through it in one piece. On most days, I was beat. I cannot pinpoint when it happened, but I do remember, wondering one day where was such rage and unhappiness coming from in one small child, and for a split second something inside of me responded, "*From you.*"

Believe it or not, it was during this very difficult phase, that I finally fell in love with my son. It still wasn't a tingly feeling, but a deep bond. A bond between two beings that endure difficulty and come out stronger in the end. I will never forget, and I gather he won't either. Looking at him with tears in my eyes, I stated, "I do not know how Nicholas, I don't understand what's happening, but Mommy is going to fight for your peace, and we will get through this." And we did. And it was during this period that I explored free will, and the constructs of control and desired behavior, of cause, and consequence and how they related to *love* and how I loved. Having explored these constructs I learned to freely love myself, and others. I am a better partner, friend, sister, mother, and daughter because of it. I am grateful for the understanding this phase produced.

By age 6, my son's rage and defiance transitioned into creativity, inquiry, and an utter abundance of energy. He evolved into an incredible life force, radiant like the sun. Fluid like water. Abundant. He was and is light. Insightful. Wise. Unapologetic. I could not help it, I was proud. Boastful. I was happy and downright grateful not just for his genius but, because our previous phase was over. Coincidentally, as proud and relieved as I was about my son's blooming personality, I have to admit, I was also bothered by how loud he was. Something about the volume of his voice and energy made me uncomfortable. He was fearless. I loved it. I still do. Yet, I found myself hushing him often, even when I enjoyed his stance. Although I knew better I dismissed this constant need to hush him as teaching him to be polite, which I viewed as good parenting on my behalf.

As it turned out, this shift in my son, paralleled a shift in my own work and creativity. Everything blossomed. As opportunities came about, fear seeped through the cracks of my self-belief. Time and time again, I kept finding myself sabotaging my own success, paralyzed by self-doubt, guilt, and shame. One day, I found myself silencing my son's inquiries and energy, this time, I was annoyed by my own habitual hushing. *"Nicholas stop it, don't be so loud,"* was quickly followed by my spirit's response, *"Why are you stopping yourself? Why do you hush yourself?"*

I finally got it. It was an audible voice to the ears of my soul. It took 6 years. Nearly every experience I had had with this child came flooding to me. I sat and closed my eyes. I took a deep breath. It was so clear to me. More than a child, he is my medium, my burning bush; how God speaks to me. I have never been surer of anything in my life. Ever. He came here to show me who I am in the world and to the world, my place in my family and community, how to embrace my authentic process. He came to teach me true happiness, what it is, what it isn't and who exactly would give it to me. He came so that I could believe in male energy and see goodness in it again; to show me how I deal with conflict resolution and control; to expose previous dysfunctional patterns, and to gift me the power of new beautiful possibilities. He taught me how to praise without production, and love without consequence; how to live loudly and manage my gifts, how to silence my fear, and turn up my gifts. He's taught me how to be my own momma and love my inner child. He came here to teach, show, and heal. To connect me to my Source… And he continues to teach and connect me daily. He is my Remembrance. Our conflicts are not conflicts, they are divine mirrors; opportunities for resolution, wisdom, and growth.

I stopped practicing religion just prior to my son being born. In Its divine grace, love, and wisdom, the Creator of all things made a sanctuary out of my home. Motherhood has not been a tingly feeling. And I no longer need it to be. Motherhood has been a spiritual experience; a journey to god-consciousness. The kind of experience they can't make cards out of to sell you stuff. The kind that changes your contribution to the space… The kind that's not even a kind but instead, one woman's story. My story.

 *Nikolai Pizarro de Jesus*

The Cycles of Motherhood

In the fall of 2015, I found myself sitting on the couch talking with my 22 year-old daughter who is pacing back and forth with words. She needed to tell me some things about her life. She began by telling me why she was in the mess she was in. She reluctantly confessed to me her troubles were caused by the thralls of her experimentation in the world of drugs. As my calm demeanor and non-reactionary response alleviated some of her anxiety, she had more to tell me but could not find the right words. Her news still synthesized with apprehension and uncertainty. She got up from the couch, ambulating from one room to the next and at one point stopped to write something on a piece of paper. I just sat quietly waiting for her to gather her thoughts. After about ten minutes, she sat down next to me again with the paper she had written clutched in her hand. I probed her to just to spit it out and she tentatively said, "You are going to be a Glam-ma" and with serenity, I said, "I know". She asked, "How did you know"? I responded, because "I am your mom."

My motherhood journey started when I was 22 years-old and I was a college student. My college years were transformative years. It was a time where my most salient identities interplayed; being Black, being a woman, being a Christian and being adopted. All of my intersections collided as I ventured into the bigger world with my innocence and naivety leading the way.

In April of 1992, I met a boy. A good man I met at church. We had a whirlwind relationship and fell in love quickly. I trusted that he loved me for who I was. I trusted he would take care of me. I trusted he was a godly man. I trusted until that one night that changed everything! My innocence and naivety did not allow me to see or discern the inner workings of his demons; alcoholism and drug abuse. Yes, I knew he struggled, but I knew he was "saved" and working on him, so things were going to be all right. Well, one night I was at his apartment waiting for him to come home. He had gone out but I had to get some studying done, so I stayed behind. He came home drunk and high, expressing how much he loved me. He assertively started kissing me while pushing me against the wall declaring his love for me. In fact, he said he loved me so much he could throw me out the ninth floor window. He continued to express his desire to make love to me but I didn't want to, I was so terribly scared. I told him, I didn't want to but he made love to me anyway as I subordinately just laid there. I took a bath afterward...

About three weeks later, I was feeling continuously nauseated and I was an emotional wreck. I couldn't concentrate in school; I dropped all my classes, my life was spiraling out of control. I was just losing it. I found out I was pregnant and I told one of my best friends. She asked me if I wanted her to *take me to the clinic*. In all my angst, I didn't even consider that as a solution.

I decided to reach out to the pastor of the church I was attending, and where we met. I went there trusting that the man of God and his wife were going to be supportive and guide me but I was wrong. The Pastor said it was my fault. He said, I didn't know a wolf in sheep's clothing and if I wasn't acting like *Jezebel*, I wouldn't be in this position. I walked away crushed, confused and alone.

I called my boyfriend and told him we needed to talk. I told him I was pregnant but could not be with him any longer. He looked at me with saddened and confused eyes and I left. I did not know how to reconcile my situation. I was in bondage. I was numb. My actions and thoughts were muddled. I couldn't rectify anything.

I dropped out of school and moved to Minneapolis. I found transitional housing for pregnant women and I applied for welfare. The welfare worker was not supportive at all. He queried my reason for leaving school to be on welfare, denounced my need for help as being a lazy Black woman and concluded I was never going to go back to school and was going to have five more kids before I was 30.

My mothering story is longer and more complex than what I have written for this piece, but it was important for me to start at the beginning and recognize the cycles in my life. I began with the story of my daughter because she is part of me and I became a mother at the time of her inception and I chose to have her. I was given a gift, and the responsibility to raise a child with all my life challenges and imperfections.

There are many conditions of my life that aren't ideal, but much of my strength comes from being a mother. My biggest responsibility in life is raising and loving my three children, and I have sacrificed a great deal to do my best. Mothering is for life. In this next cycle, my job is to support my daughter as she enters into motherhood journey.

Anonymous Black Lotus Mother

Labor Pains

I labored over her body
But neglected to labor over her soul
I miscarried the perception of the total person as a
whole

My heart skipped a beat
It didn't repeat after Him
The rhythm of His constant love
But at times remained still
And...

Born was the seed of
Hatred and self-will
To live
Was anything ill of pleasure
And if I were to measure
the length of happiness on the scale
It would go from 1 to one day I will be genuinely
happy to be a girl
To offer everything I have
To this cruel and gentle world

But the pains!!!!
Prematurely postponed was the breath of life
That was cut off by the cords of
Discord
AND
Strangled by the strains of strife

PUSH!!
Pray until something happens
Until the cords are loosed

And the manifestation of life is in action

PUSH!!
Pray unit something happens
Until His joy is flowing through the veins of the one
who was once saddened

PUSH!!!
Pray until something happen
Until...
Something happens
Until..............
Something... happened

 ***Desiree R. Flowers***

No title for my life... I just have a purpose?

What is your definition of strength? Being strong to many is an option, no I am not the one to knock anyone for giving in or bowing out of their struggles because each of us are who we are, but for me being strong wasn't something I chose to do, it was something I HAD to do for my children. My journey as a mother has been like no other; of course this is my opinion, although many can relate on many of the levels to what I've endured. I consider many of my hardships and pains to be lessons of hard, raw truth. Mine is a testimony if you want one, that's for sure. You see, I've endured the type of pain that somehow haunts you, no matter how much therapy or positive advice. No matter if you are people who are relatable or reputable models, you may have given in to the need to keep it all inside, to vent, or whatever.

Yes, I've cried endless days and I've screamed until my screams were inaudible, but I heard them just as loud in my head. Yes, I've prayed; I mean who can honestly say that if you are one of faith in a higher being that you haven't prayed during trying times? So, what I'm trying to convey here to you is that, *THE PAIN LIVES HONEY! IT LIVES! IT LIVES!!!!!!* However, I believe that time has definitely taught me to endure and manage how that pain is radiated, but even still, triggers are very real, and I believe in my mind and heart that in the same breath when I say this, "triggers are a blessing and also a curse." Not sure if I need to expound on that or not, but again that's my opinion.

I became a mother by the time I was 17. I was ultimately looking for love in hopeless places. I was not attracted to that man. I didn't desire him. I didn't want a family because I was trying to become someone and make something out of my life, but at the same time, I was proud when I found out I was pregnant because I gained all of those things with someone who wanted that and more with me at the time. I barely graduated from high school, but I did. I didn't have to struggle or take the more difficult road to make that happen. Despite ALL of this, I still graduated!

Before I conceived my first child, I was raped by some random guy who made me the eye of his desires within a matter of minutes. He followed me, and the next thing I remember is waking up from being passed out in someone else's apartment (not his) and him pretending he had a weapon behind my back, me pissing my pants and him walking me inches from my door and pretending that we were somehow dating, to keep me from crying the moment I hit my doorstep, and having my mother and brother run out after his goofy ass to kill him. My brother went one way looking for him searching hard, and moms called the police and they rushed me to the hospital to get, not my first rape kit done in my life, but, yes… my second. So now I ask, what is your definition of being victimized? I did not want to be viewed as a victim I just wanted it all to go away, I wanted it to never happen, I could have done without the sympathy talks and stares and cares for me. I wished more that it didn't have to disturb my capacity to trust people. I wanted, to a great extent, to fill the void I was missing. That's it, that's all.

Several months after I was raped, *I forced myself to make love* to my children's father, and I gave him a child. I was pregnant in court pointing out my attacker, with him beside me for moral support. Can you imagine how that looked? I was embarrassed and I felt ashamed. Why? I didn't ask for that to happen to me, I didn't have "rape me" written on my ass as I walked away that night. I owned my truth though, knowing somehow I was gonna bounce back, because I had been there before. When my eldest brother's two close friends molested me at the age of 7 I received the help and support I needed from members of my mother's church. I guess it was effective, the older I got the more I came to the conclusion that that shit was only meant to keep me from crying. I am pretty sure my mom believed in faith and the church more than she did the therapist, which was okay to a certain extent, but she wasn't accepting the idea that some therapist could help me more than her prayers and support from the ministry.

Well, that substance wasn't enough, because all I did was block the experience out of my consciousness. I wasn't necessarily afraid to speak about it, I just wanted it blocked from my psyche, to be protected from triggers, and from fear of living average. I am not saying that the church people's invocations didn't help, but my soul desired more, I just didn't know what it was exactly. I just knew in my heart that *I wasn't entirely okay*. Now that I reflect on it, I was experiencing Post-Traumatic Stress Disorder (PTSD), which is "a mental health condition triggered by experiencing or seeing a terrifying event," it ultimately can have never-ending effects on your life, anxiety plagues you at any given time.

Fast forwarding on my parenting journey, for the most part I was afraid of it, not because of uncertainties about whether I could get the job done or not, but because of the man I made a decision to father my children with. He made me feel inadequate even when I felt superior in other areas of my life. Like, I was one of the best moms in the world, because I did well for my kids. I nourished, clothed, taught, encouraged, guided, provided for them…but the one thing if you noticed I did not say, was be the best role model I could and I tried. Don't get me wrong, the Lord knows I tried, but the man I never was utterly in love with and offered 12 years of my life to, just made it hard. Wretchedly, I allowed him to control me and I allowed way too much. I fought back, yes physically more times than a few, but I fought more so for my emotions, and my rights as a mother more than anything. And, for that I felt decisions and better judgment could've been in my favor if I fought harder, and cried and begged less. I took the good and the bad days with him in strides, and after a few proposals for marriage it was clear I did not care about the scars he left on me, both emotional and physical.

I now reflect on all the times my boys cried and every time they saw the abuse happening. I matched it with countless reminders and counsels with them about forgiving him and promising me they wouldn't one day mimic their father's ways. I remember sitting my oldest son down and asking him questions about what he would do if the situations came up in his relationships one day with his wife or girlfriends. I would make sure he knew that this was never okay. It wasn't until my fourth child (my only daughter) was born that I started valuing and understanding her feelings that things shifted. Those were the moments I decided I should pay more attention to my kids and what they felt about what they saw and heard. She made that difference; I was ashamed that it took her to be put in the mix for me to put a stop to the abuse. She was the only one of my children that displayed how much it hurt her to see this happening, although there was one more child born after her, my baby boy. As my daughter aged she screamed, she yelled, she made him promise he would stop hurting me and sometimes he listened.

The day he stopped caring about her feelings was the day I knew I needed to leave for good. Yes, there was enough gumption in me to leave plenty of times within the 12+ years, although obviously I went back, but I swear I felt liberated each time. When we finally separated for good, I had to make a decision I wasn't prepared for that altered my life beyond words. He was a good father to the kids when we weren't arguing or fighting, a man who never left or walked away from them a day in either of their lives. I soon became the breadwinner, bringing the only income and education to the table. I allowed this because he was not receiving any income due to his disability after having a major stroke, which caused him to rely on dialysis. I felt it was deserved -

his own karma from all I endured during the course of our relationship.

At one point, I allowed him to move my children over 70 miles away from where I was staying with my grandmother to attempt to give them a better education and room to grow. I never questioned whether he could do it; I just couldn't trust that he would love me like he promised even after he knew I was never coming to him. My Grandmother told me he had assured her that he would always take care of his kids in a conversation, she said; "he never said anything about you". I never understood why she interpreted that from him, but now I do. He took my kids and for 3 years I allowed him to co-parent with me, and I made myself believe everything was going good with my babies and they were in good hands.

At the time, I was still paralyzed from fear, and I was afraid to face charges because I had not completed probation requirements, that led to law enforcement putting an arrest warrant out on me. For years I didn't hide from the law, but I didn't turn myself in either and I knew he would use it against me so he made my kids his pawns against me. I didn't want to have to go away from my babies so I allowed him to continue to hurt me through them. I wish I understood I didn't have much to be scared of. I wish I knew that not having a previous rap sheet would have been beneficial on my behalf; I wish I knew the law would have been more in my favor if I had not been afraid. I wish I knew what I know now. After seven years the law finally captured me. I ended up spending four and a half months away from the world. Although I wouldn't recommend jail to anyone, that was the happiest, liberating months of my life. I was free to fight him.

Although we were getting along better than when we first met, I didn't know all that time my children were subjects of his abuse, pain, and his agony of realizations of never being able to have me to make his family whole again.

He abused them and hid it from me. He made them suffer every time I pissed him off. He mercilessly beat my kids scared, mainly the oldest three boys received torture they didn't deserve, until one day he took it too far… He beat my three boys so badly that he took the life of my precious 2nd oldest child.

 I miss my son more than anything in this entire world; it hurts to live, it hurts to celebrate, it hurts to know he will never come back, but the rawest truth is knowing I haven't woke up one day in the four years he's been gone without him on my mind. I have lived through some extremely difficult ass days that I just try to remember to breathe between the screams and until other memories take over. I just know to keep living for the children, and I am learning that more every day. After this tragedy, living is the single greatest challenge for me, but it's because of my surviving children I continue to do this. I honestly don't really want people to be sad for me, but I would rather leave a mark in some one's life and be their stimulus to make changes before it is too late. I get choked up when my kids tell me things they admire about me, and when they tell me those wonderful "I love mommy because" proclamations--- only because I don't believe it when hearing it. I am getting it more and more as I enjoy motherhood and there isn't anything I wouldn't do (within reason) for them.

 My children are amazing. I am not saying this just because they are "my children," but they are literally walking, breathing, everyday ordinary heroes. The things they have endured and the obstacles they have experienced would make the wildest of wild imaginations second-guess their own life experiences. I tell them all the time I need them more than they need me. My children will be great people one day and I know it. So, until they make it to their prospective places in this life, I will continue to watch them and allow them to inspire me, and let our Angel in heaven push us beyond limits.

What do I title this again I ask? I'm just living because He gave me a purpose. Thank you God for my purpose! To all the Queens, walk in your purpose, own your truth, especially when you are living THROUGH it. When you refuse to be blinded, you become less of a victim, and you start taking back whatever was stolen from you. If you haven't taken anything I have said into account, I hope you can at the least tell or share this with someone else who may be in a similar situation. When you see how someone else can be inspired by your situation, then it becomes beneficial to you.

Blessings. Ashe.

Tiffany Townsend

Made Out of Love

My Childhood was great, no complaints... at least from a child's point of view. My parents were a happily married couple, but my dad was and still is a functioning alcoholic. He never put his hands on my mom or anything like that, but he cheated and just like that it was over. My mother got custody of me, and I only saw my father on weekends. My father is a Vietnam Vet who came back and got a good job working for Amtrak. He has an awesome sense of humor and avoids confrontations, especially with women. His heart is always in the right place, but the generational curse of alcoholism has a strong hold on him. I know for a fact when he messed his family up that he went into a deep depression.

I was only three when it was explained to me, so it didn't bother me until I got older and realized I grew up chasing after the wrong men because they complimented me. I was pretty on the outside, and some even considered me to be really spoiled growing up because even though my parents weren't together you could tell they loved me. Eventually my father remarried and our relationship suffered and unfortunately, so did I. Not saying I didn't want my parents to move on, but my stepmother made a lot of things hard for me. I had to defend myself a lot and I don't know if my dad noticed or even cared.

My mother, on the other hand, is the epitome of a strong Black woman. She worked as a correctional officer and didn't take anyone's shit. It may sound cliché or even biased, but I love her. She's been there for me all my life, and she's definitely my role model. Whenever my dad didn't come through she always had my back. I don't hate my father or anything, we always had a strong bond, but he did hurt me and there was always a void in my life as a result of his absence. So, I grew up being taught not to depend on a man, guys only want one thing, blah, blah, blah, but of course I was boy crazy even though I didn't lose my virginity until I was in college, but I was still trying to fill that void.

I've been through my fair share of crazy relationships too! I've been cheated on way too many times, experienced domestic violence, etc. I know my mother didn't raise me to endure that, but I didn't know my worth. I met my husband on a random night at a barbeque that neither one of us was planning to attend. Even though we had our pasts, we both were there for each other. He has always been patient with me because I have a fragile heart. It's been broken so many times that I lost some of the pieces, and he's willing to help me find them or create new ones. Of course, with his parents still being together, there is a lot he can teach me about love, relationships and marriage for that matter. And of course I don't ever want a divorce so there is a lot of work to be done.

After five years together and three married, I found out I was pregnant. My pregnancy was something I didn't know how to feel about. Ultimately, I had mixed emotions. Of course I wanted a child with my husband, but I was not where I wanted to be in life. I had just graduated college, moved to a different state, and neither of us had jobs and we lived with my mother.

Upon hearing the news, I was quietly freaking out because I have always been told that moms get stuck with the children majority of the time. I didn't know what to teach this child, I was going through my own pains, fears, and struggles, etc. Now, someone was going to be looking at me, learning from me, and listening to me. Scary feeling. But God had us the whole time. After the initial shock of finding out I was pregnant, I was ecstatic.

I was convinced I was going to break the generational curses of my family. I wanted *her* to be born into a loving environment. No anger, no regret, no bad vibes, no drama, NONE OF IT! Even though I had to have a C-section because she was breached, it was an awesome experience that I'll never forget. Kharmai (meaning noble and anointed) has brightened so many things in my life; now I truly know what love is. My husband found an awesome job, we got a house and I was able to be a stay at home mom for a while.

Areas that were dark and gray I can see clearer now, and I don't want to share or have any of that negativity with her. Our pasts should not interfere with her future. I don't think my father ever meant to hurt me, but looking at my child I don't know how he did it. No matter how bad or messed up a situation may be, adults still need take care of their responsibilities and still be present of the children and families. Your decisions no longer only affect you.

Three months after giving birth, the ugly demon of Postpartum Depression hit me really hard like a ton of bricks. I felt like I was on top of the world when I was pregnant and all of sudden, I started feeling extremely low. I experienced having no self-confidence, feeling jealous of others, visions of me killing my child, crying spells, and much more. I was in denial until I had those visions and I went and got professional help. After I was diagnosed, I was prescribed medication and I hated the medication because I didn't feel like myself and the worse part of all was I had to stop breastfeeding Mai. I got some courage and strength four months later, and I promised myself that if I flushed the pills down the toilet I would be fine. I knew I would be fine. No one's perfect. That was over a year ago, and even though I have my moments I've definitely come a long way.

I've always wanted to let women know that all races have PPD. I was in denial about it because you grow up with society making it seem like Black women don't have mental disorders or struggle with mental health, but it's not true. Get help, but don't make it a crutch. I got off the medication when I was ready, not because of what others may have thought. My main objective was, and still is my daughter and her happiness, and that makes every day a lot easier.

 **LaSharra Jackson-Merriweather**

A Letter to My Doodle

I **always said I would never have**

children, so I tried to fill my life with travel, food, and good people. Motherhood was undesirable and it represented abandonment, unfulfilled dreams and the ultimate failure. All my negative connotations may have stemmed from my absent father, or the abortion I had while searching for a boy to replace him. Or the neglect I experienced when my mother and I had a falling out due to my decision to no longer be the built-in babysitter for my younger siblings I helped raise for the latter part of my life. Our dispute resulted in us not speaking for almost a year.

During my transition from teenager to adulthood, I got the abortion because I just knew I couldn't bring someone I loved into a world this cold. But somewhere along the line I changed my mind about bearing children. Maybe it was when I heard your heartbeat for the first time or during the 3D ultrasound when I saw your side profile. Either way, I knew the world would be better because you were in it. While I thought I would be the one to help raise and guide you along your lifelong journey you have taught me so much already. I have learned to enjoy the moment because all your first experiences only happen once. I learned that I no longer have to keep up this façade of perfection - every time I think I am dressed to the nines, and you decide your sticky hands need to grab my leg to coax me to raise you up for our daily hugs.

I have learned that in order to love you and anyone else unconditionally I have to love myself. After giving birth I hated my body. Filled with stretch marks, it was not the idea of perfection that society or my family told me I should portray. It took me 14 months to appreciate my tiger stripes because not all women have the luxury of motherhood. I have learned that I am worthy of love and not just any kind of love, but that agape love.

I have learned that asking for help doesn't make me weak it makes me smart. No one expects me to wear my superwoman cape 24/7, and I wish I knew this when you were born because it would have saved me from months of isolation and silent depression. It would have saved me from wondering why no one came to visit after the first few days of my weeklong stint in the hospital after my cesarean where I had to force myself to walk again through unbearable abdominal pain. Or why no one came to check on me, except for your paternal grandmother and maternal grandfather when I got home. Yes, your grandfather and I have reconciled, and I needed this reconciliation in order to allow your father to love me and I to love him. I thank the Creator for your father because he was there every step of the way even washing my ass when I couldn't.

Fast-forward a little over a year after your birth, thank you because your birth has fostered a friendship between my mother and I that I yearned for the majority of my life. Through the experiences with my parents, it is best that although you may view me through idealized eyes please don't, I am your parental figure, raising a princess that will ultimately be a lifelong friend in your *queendom*. Appreciate your family because you only have one and you are surrounded by love from your father, older brothers, grandparents, great-grandparents, aunts, uncles, and cousins. Dream big, bigger than you could imagine – because you may one day create someone/ something as great, or even greater than you. I admit I'm slightly biased because

I can't see anyone being greater than you, because you're MY baby!

Love Mama (Catrice Carter)

Untitled

As I look back on the last thirty-two years as a mother it never dawned on me, something that was the only thing I ever felt I would be good at would have been the most difficult thing I ever did and continue to do…

As a mother of eight, one step, four biological and three adopted children, the last 22 years have been very difficult. So difficult, in fact when people ask me for advice I often have to refrain from saying, "NO! Stop and think twice before you become a parent."

I remember as a child playing house and always wanting to have a load of children, and when my husband and I talked about kids he always told me he wanted a basketball team full as well. My first child was born before my husband and I were married but that didn't matter to me. I was the happiest when I was with my baby girl. I was happy during my pregnancy, and the delivery wasn't even difficult. She came out two days after school had ended for the summer, so it was the perfect time in my book, except I was so broke that I had to go back to work two weeks after she was born. That summer I would take her, and set her in her infant seat on a table right in the middle of the class.

Those first years of motherhood, though very hard with long hours at work and being in school, were the best ever. You see, I was meant to be a mother and I practiced all the things you were told to do to become one, including keeping schedules, arranging play dates and making sure my children were surrounded by positive influences in their lives. Life was good, their father was an amazing father who always believed the best thing he could give his children was love, and to help support their mother. And he did just that, even when I suggested adopting a child from one of Minnesota's Waiting Children. We will talk about that a little bit later. Right now I want to share one of the most difficult memories of giving birth to my youngest biological child.

Twenty-five years ago this week, I went into labor nine days before my due date which wasn't too uncommon. Two of my children were born a couple days early but this one was different. I went into labor one evening while watching the Fresh Prince's TV show. My husband wasn't home, so I called him and told him something was wrong, and I needed to get to the hospital right away. We were living in Atlanta, far from my parents so we had to get a neighbor to come and sit with the other kids that were 2, 4 and 6 at the time. By the time we got to the hospital I was in full-blown labor. Within one hour I was ready to push but there were no doctors around, so my husband and the nurse delivered my son. All I remember was my husband telling the nurse something was wrong. The umbilical cord was wrapped around his neck. After several minutes they had remedied the situation and he let out a huge wail. However, this was the beginning of many difficult days for him. Following this difficult birth came many difficult diagnosis including ADHD and finally Asperger Syndrome, which is high functioning Autism. With this diagnosis came my never ending search for how to make all children's learning experiences less difficult when they are born with different abilities, and those who don't fall in the "normal" category, or according to what the rest of the world considers normal.

Through the years that have followed, parenting my son has been hard at times and requires much prayer. It wasn't until many years later, and three more children that I questioned my parenting skills.

I am a true believer that everything happens for a reason, but for the life of me I couldn't understand why certain people insist on bringing children into this world only to have them taken away time and time again. My adopted daughters were born to a mother who has had eight children all of whom were removed from her custody by the time they were a year old. Each child was brought into this world with a deficit, either drug addiction and/or mental illness. Again, I trusted God to give me what I needed to parent my hurting children, and nineteen years later I have to continue to pray for strength. My girls struggle day in and day out with mental health, attachment and abandonment issues. It constantly angers me that they have to struggle with these issues, but again I am reminded these are things that make us stronger are needed to mode us into the people we are intended to be.

Now as a grandmother of five, it wasn't until my last grandchild was born that I realized how awesome it is to see your own child bring a child into the world. You see, when my stepdaughter had her children we were living in another part of the country, so I wasn't involved in their early life. But, four years ago my daughter delivered the most beautiful grandson with the greatest spirit anyone could ever ask for.

As a single mom, my daughter lived with us for my grandson's first years of life. We felt the need to support her so we gave her an hour of alone time each evening. From his first week of life we would lay him in between us each night and sing to him, "King Ali handsome is he Alibaba." Now, he is four years old and when he spends the night with "G-ma and Papa," as he calls us, he jumps in the bed between us and asks us to sing to him. As I watch my daughter raise her son, and my stepdaughter's teenage daughter, I feel so blessed to have parented such wonderful, loving and caring children.

My dream is to continue to support and nurture not only my own daughters to be great mothers, but other women who I may come in contact with. What I have found is being a mother, as difficult as it may be, can also be one of the greatest gifts from God.

Ann Johnson, the Village Mother

Critical Transitions of Woman/Mother(hood): Late, But Just in Time for Conception

My wise midwife once told me, "the aborted seed tries to return and some do find their way back." We have many encounters in life that we never forget, even silent ones. In a past transition of womanhood, I'm in college, frantically rushing out of my studio apartment in the hood and I'm late for class as usual. But, I still choose to walk, not take the bus. I just stroll fast through the West End. In my daze, I notice a young boy coming into view. He's shining like the sun is right over him. We are walking towards each. Even from a distance, we lock eyes and keep walking towards one another. He had such a brilliant smile; all I could do is start smiling back. It seemed the closer we got to each other, the brighter his smile, the more radiant I begin to feel. I felt flushed; some strange energy exerted itself over me. I don't think we stopped but we kept our eyes locked on each other. Even though I was late and stressed, I feel lifted. We pass each other and after a few feet we turn around, pause, walk backward, still smiling, still staring deeply, we turn back to our opposite paths and continue our opposite journeys.

I thought about him all day, why wasn't he in school, should I have stopped and asked if he needed help? No, no, he didn't seem distressed in any way. He knew where he was going, right? Yeah, he was sure of his destination. He was a ray of light. Out of all the things I've encountered in life, this is one of my most vivid memories. You're late but just in time, just in time for a moment, unknown of internal happenings.

Transition into motherhood…

As a mother, there is a point when you feel fulfilled. Two daughters? Yes. A son and daughter would have been ideal, but two daughters…my mother has two daughters. It's good. The baby girl is becoming a big girl, she can put her shoes on by herself, and my big girl is such a leader. I'm fulfilled. My body is my own again. I'll have no son; it's good, Quanda and her daughters…

Transitions of woman/mother(hood)…I want to leave this man…

I'm good. I got my daughters. I can raise daughters with or without him, and I'm fulfilled. I can move back to Georgia, and I can raise these daughters with my mom, sister, and aunties. I'm good, I can do this, I can leave this frozen tundra, and I can go back and get a Master's degree. There could be warm weather, Black people, culture, everything as before but two daughters in tow. Yes, it's time...

I'm late! Well, it is what it is...I'm pregnant again. I'm old, and I don't want to do this again. The youngest baby girl is becoming a big girl, she can put her shoes on by herself, and my big girl is such a leader. Why, did I let this happen? I must be dumb as hell. I was leaving him and this state, right? I'm not going to do this, no, I'm not, and I'm too old for this shit... I'm done!

We talked and he's very disappointed, but he understands. I called to make an appointment but I have to wait because we have already planned to go down south for a family reunion. I'm just so mad at myself, why did I let this happen? The appointment is the day after our return. Just do this trip no worries; we're good... you're good Quanda. This will be over, is what I kept telling myself.

I can't do this, I just can't. I had too much time to think about it. I'm pro-choice, but I can't do this. Why would I do this? I have a decent job, another baby is not going to send us off the edge, into the projects and make me get hooked on crack or something. No nothing like that at all. I don't want another baby, I don't. I want me. Before was different, I was in college, I was young, and I was not really with the father. I can't do this, I'm pro-choice, but I didn't handle it well many moons ago. No, not well at all… years of regret, uncertainty, and sadness. It took me so long to even get pregnant again. He asked me not to do it. My midwife said she would raise the baby, this unwanted, unplanned, bonus baby.

I don't feel pregnant, so weird. Everyone is excited at work; I'm like the fourth woman in a row to get pregnant. We joke about the curse of the job! I go through the motions; this is strange because I don't feel pregnant at all, not like my pregnancies with the girls. What if it's another girl and another head of hair to do? I'll leave them all, just run away; why am I doing this?

We do an ultrasound and it's a man-child. I remember that shining walking boy with the brilliant smile. Was he real? I don't recall anyone on the street, any cars on the road that day, just him and I. Was that a real moment? Who was that little boy? Oh wait, I know who he was, he's coming back. I'm relieved, I know this baby. Throughout the years I've calculated what his age would be. Weeks go by, I don't roll up to my desk the same, there's the bulge of my sun. I accept the pregnancy, but I'm suffering silently inside, I really didn't want another baby, I just wanted me. I only share this with my midwife, she still offers to raise the baby, but his father would never let that happen and it's a man-child.

My mother buys me a gorgeous pair of gold earrings and an iPod; these are labor gifts. I laugh, these earrings are the only things I'm going to wear in labor! I'm anxious and excited, and things feel right.

The midwife has been here for about two weeks; she came early to help with the girls while I finish up my last weeks of work. I just want this to be over. I won with the name Sundjata, *Lion Warrior,* but I lost with the circumcision battle. I will have an uncircumcised sun. The midwife convinced his father there was no purpose for it. I'm just like really - you are, your brothers are, your older sons are, who's gonna be explaining to him how to properly clean himself, probably my ass. It's whatever, I guess... I'm too old for this shit...

I wake up on Thursday, February 19th, 2009 and I'm in labor… I'm too old for this shit…I'm trying to show no hint of anything to the girls and they're looking at me funny. We get them ready for school, they are six and four now. As I look out the window at them getting on the bus I think, *it's never gonna be the same after today.*

Hours later… I'm trying, but I'm so tired. I swear I push and push, he's crowning, but the moment I take one little breather, he slides back up into my birth canal. What the hell!? I'm so tired. I try again, the same thing happens. I finally, use my last of everything- will, breath, strength, to push him out, he has caul over his face. I look at him, but I just want to sleep. The girls come home from school and we begin our new reality.

The midwife leaves a few days after the birth, and I'm alone with this little being. When I reflect now, I can't remember anything I was feeling then, nothing. I let him sleep, I try to nurse him, but he falls asleep, and I just let him sleep, and don't wake him up to nurse every two hours. I know he's tired because he traveled hard and far, so I don't disturb him. I check in with my midwife, but I don't remember her words, *maybe something* like "he's jaundice for sure, yellowish eyes".

I *do* remember moving his cradle near the window for sunlight. The days continue to go by, and I just look at him sleep a lot. He sleeps and it's the same routine; I try to nurse him, he latches for a bit falls asleep for four to five long hours. Were the girls like this? Something is wrong with this baby. He's about three weeks and looks so much smaller than before--- like I see his ribs, he looks gray and his urine is extremely dark. One night I'm holding him, I tell his father, "something's wrong, look at him," he asked me if he was breathing…I'm blank, he tells me "you need to feed him."

The next day, I pull myself together, and I go buy a baby digital scale. We weigh him that evening, and although this baby was born eight pounds and four ounces, he is *barely six pounds!* Something about seeing actual numbers pulled me back to reality swiftly. What the fuck Quanda?! What the fuck is wrong with you?! Why are you not feeding your baby Sun properly?! I snapped, I'm crying, the girls are looking at me crazy, this weak baby is looking at me, their father is looking at me, and my ancestors are looking at me. I'm a fucked up individual. I call the midwife; I don't even know what I'm saying. I just think the baby is going to die. She's telling me I got to get my milk back up and strong, change my diet, and she's giving a list of things to try to increase my supply and raise the fat content of his milk. I hear her minimally, but what I hear from within is "Go get this baby some formula." I tell his father and he's like go. So I rush to the nearest co-op, grab an organic soy formula and some Mother's Milk Tea, I rush home, I prepare the formula and I prepare the tea, both of which are mixed with tears. I feed him formula from a bottle and he greedily suckles every ounce of the concoction. At this point, he's four weeks and looks newly premature to me. Both of my girls were born over nine pounds and just got Buddha fat from my milk, so in comparison this small boy looked so frail.

The next weeks were a true struggle, I worked to get my milk up, tried different formulas, tried different homemade mixtures, but the weight was so slow to improve. People from work wanted to see him but I was too embarrassed to reveal him to the world. I just couldn't believe I was this ill-fit mother. Unfortunately, Sundjata never became a chubby baby, toddler or little boy. It wasn't until years later when a good friend had a baby and told me about her experience with postpartum depression, that I came to realize that's what I went through. This realization just led to more ill feelings. I was so smart, but so dumb, to not know what was going on, or to seek proper help to be the best mother I could be for my *Sun*. I never got my milk right so Sundjata was breastfeed for comfort, but nutrients were supplemented by formula. He was the only one of my kids that I went back to work full-time after twelve weeks of maternity leave. As a result of this, I still carry so much guilt.

I've just started acknowledging and talking about postpartum depression, because it's a very tender moment from my past. As Black women, we try to be so strong and carry so much on our shoulders, and often times we don't hold ourselves accountable for being vulnerable or acknowledging that mental health issues exist in our community as well.

But my Sun came back, like his name he is a warrior, he survived almost being re-aborted and starving. So many times I look at him and I can't even believe I'm his mother. There are times he'll do something or say something deep that is way beyond his age and I'll calculate his true age, and he's still wiser than that, and it makes so much sense. He made his way back. He's meant to make changes in this world, and I realize nurturing his soul and his sisters' is my most essential duty, and I'm blessed they chose me.

 *Quanda Arch*

"A Journey to the Unknown"

Me being so young,
So precious and innocent myself,
I had no idea you were real.
I did not know what it meant
To be "with child."
My body didn't change at all
Early on
Sweet 16 with a stomach
That was as flat as a board,
So when the doctor said 4 months
I couldn't accept his words as truth.
Struck with fear and ignorance
My life flashed before my eyes.
One day I planned a life with you,
On other days I plotted my escape.
The God in me told me not to worry, pray
And trust in God's plan.
Society, fear, and others told me to think about how
awful my future would be, if I still had one at all.
I was torn.
Torn between the real me,
The loving and God-fearing me,
And the young, scared, and fragile me.
When I arrived to the location, people blocked the
entrance holding boards with dead babies plastered all
over them.
They warned me,
They cried,
They even begged me,
"Stop, don't kill your baby!'
I was terrified!
I remember thinking,
"but I'm not killing my baby. Am I?"

I was uncertain and in denial.
I entered the room and hopped up on the table,
Unsure what would happen next.
The first step was something called an ultrasound.
Something I had never had before.
They placed cold jelly on my belly, and an instrument attached to a computer by a cord.
The doctor asked, "Do you want to see? It's okay if you don't want to, because most women don't want to."
I replied, out of curiosity, anxiousness, and disbelief, "Yes I want to see."
She turned the monitor around and there you were!
As clear as day,
A baby!
She pointed to the monitor, "This is the spine."
"What is that?" I asked.
"That's the baby's heart." The doctor answered.
I looked at my belly and yelled, "That's in there?
Where is it in there?
Shouldn't my belly be big?" My eyes were the size of golf balls.
"That's a baby!" I yelled again. "A real baby!"
I looked at the doctor with my mouth to the floor,
"I didn't know it was a real person with a heartbeat. Heartbeats mean it's alive!"
"Yes," the doctor said.
I remember being confused at that point. I knew I was at a clinic, but not just any clinic I realized.
The doctor said, "You are 19 weeks pregnant."
I then asked, "Well, what will you do to the baby? How will you get it out?"
The doctor explained, like it was routine, "I'm going to insert these pins inside you to open your cervix. You will have to leave, and then come back tomorrow. When you

return, I will use a type of vacuum instrument to suck the baby out piece by piece."

Awkward stares.

Awkward silence.

I just knew she did not say what she said with a straight face,

And it hit me like a bus.

Bewildered I spoke, "So you all kill babies here? That's what's happening. You explained it in a way that made it sound normal. This is a baby. If you suck his arms and legs off he will be hurt and he will cry. You're going to rip my baby a part piece by piece?"

A question but not really a question.

It was more like clarification and understanding.

A light bulb moment.

Awkward stares.

Awkward silence.

"No thanks! I yelled. "I don't know what I'm going to do, but you are not killing my baby! It's my baby!"

At that moment,

Consciously I became that baby's mother.

Ever since then, I have been his mom.

Me being a baby myself, I had no idea what being a mother meant.

I couldn't even begin to imagine the magnitude of the obstacles I would face ahead.

The only thing I knew was that I was protecting that baby by any means necessary

Even, if that meant doing it alone.

There was no greater love than meeting him for the first time.

In fact, before that moment

I did not know what true love was.

An example of how much God loved me,

To bless me with perfection, unconditional love

A lifelong blessing
There have been days when I've felt unworthy and unfit.
There have been days when I gave up hope.
There has been a SEA of tears,
Guilt, regret, shame, and mistakes,
But!
My days have also been filled with love,
Innocent unconditional God-like love
And forgiveness, smiles, and joy,
Happiness,
And everyday blessings!
I get to look into the dreamiest eyes.
Eyes filled with divine purpose!
Eyes with the brightest twinkle!
Eyes that are proof that something greater than I exists,
And is in control.
All the money in the world couldn't buy this!
I love him more than life itself!
8.30.05
The day my perfect gift from God arrived.
The choice was mine, and mine alone to make.
With all certainty I knew his life was not mine to take.
Because a gift *so pure* could never be a mistake.

 Cassie Dodd

The Black Woman Complex

I died…
And I seen the light I felt her open up wide exactly 3 times
as a thief in the night
Despite my awareness of life I felt like I was dying...

As my womb opened up the portal of her universe.
I felt the curse

Why am I describing labor pains equivalent to death,
Yes?
Why am I broken when I'm feeling neglected,
Yes?
Why do the words seem to never reflect?
Yes?

Best way to explain is that…
I say too much
Love too much
Hurt too much
But it's never enough

Have you ever felt 52 bones shatter in your body at the
same time?
I have

As my lips struggled to grip the straw thirsting for water
I must of felt all the pain that my Black boys would feel
through their lifetime
Shhhh. Don't say such words
I must of felt all the pain of my mother's mother, and other
mothers through labor.

Everyone got here through her womb.

Everyone has a mom, the thought that everyone came from
somewhere…

But, it's painful...
Did I fail as a mother?
I often felt the needs of my children were being selfishly
ignored from my unstable mind.
Somehow trying to figure out how to be a mother when I
was still...a child

No one is ever completely ready to become a parent
Parenting comes from experience.
The experience of having to clean up after a party you were
never invited to.
Or walking to the bathroom in the middle of the night
almost breaking your ankle stepping on a Ninja Turtle
action figure.

I love my boys
They're one manifestation of me
Of us.
Mom & Dad.
God.
Gratitude:
The quality of being thankful; readiness to show
appreciation for and to return kindness
Have I've shown enough gratitude for such a gift as this?
I Am Thankful.

Being a mom is patience.

The ability to turn a penny into gold
Ascended alchemist from a generation of healers,
astrologers, doulas, midwives, and medicine
wombman.

When I realized I was in pain.
I desperately needed space to heal as a woman.
Things weren't going great within my interpersonal
relationships, I became alone...
In the midst of a crowded room
How did I cope?

I'm still coping
By living life, spending time with my children
Showing Gratitude

I Died
And I seen the light
And The Light was the opening of my womb
My Birth Right

 *Claire Lyrics*

Untitled

I never wanted to have children. I've always considered myself somewhat of a free spirit, and wanted to be able to roam the world whenever I wanted. I grew up in a family with five sisters and two brothers. So I always figured I'd be the world's best aunt if nothing else. I enjoyed the idea of sleeping when I wanted. Being single and exploring the options of having any man I wanted. Most importantly, I would enjoy traveling the world with no particular place in mind.

I moved back to Minnesota after living in Charlotte, NC for 10 years. Two weeks after I moved back I started dating an older man. Four months after I moved back I found out I was pregnant by this older man. When I told him, he told me he would be there for me. I didn't hear from him though, not unless I called him. He always made me feel like I was inconveniencing him when I called. So I stopped calling.

Over the next few months I did everything necessary to take care of myself and my baby. I went to the doctor's appointments. I researched ways to nourish myself and my child because I was so sick all the time. I cried myself to sleep night after night because I no longer had the support promised to me by my child's father. I cried because I was alone, and my child was being born into a broken family. I was slipping into depression and there was nothing I could do to stop myself. My friends and family were very supportive, however I didn't have the support from the one person I craved it from, the person who helped me create this life. I felt abandoned.

When it was time for my son to be born I was as ready as I thought I could be. I had money saved up, my parents allowed me to setup their dining room for my son and I, and I had everything I needed to be comfortable as a first time mommy. Still, I was depressed. I was mean. I was sad. I hated the thought of having to take care of this child by myself because I felt like I shouldn't have to. I hated my son's father was able to continue on with his life uninterrupted. I still cried myself to sleep every night. But I was ready. I made up my mind that I was going to do any and everything to make sure my child's life was the most amazing I could offer.

My labor was induced because of high blood pressure. I was ready for him to get out of my body though. I hated being pregnant. I checked into the hospital, and when my mom called my son's father he said to call him when it was time. When it was time, he came to the hospital. He didn't touch me, he didn't tell me it would be okay or that he was there for me, he didn't say thank you for birthing his child or tell me I was beautiful. Instead he stood in the bathroom peeking out through the door. And when Ali made his debut into the world, he wouldn't take the scissors to cut the umbilical cord, so I cut it myself, this would be symbolic of the parenting journey, I had ahead of me. And when the midwife handed me my baby, I felt this energy and feeling of complete calm and happiness. I cried some more, but this time it was tears of pure joy. I couldn't believe I made this person. I couldn't believe God chose me to be the mom of the most perfect thing I'd ever laid my eyes on. I was in the deepest most pure kind of love.

I left the hospital a few days later and I was still feeling depressed. Ali's dad had been to see us once. It was for about 30 minutes and he slept in the hospital chair the whole time. I knew he wasn't going to be much help as a co-parent at that moment. I should have come to terms with it, but, I didn't. Not until about a month later. Ali's dad had been to see him a few times a week. He would stay for about 30 minutes, gag when it was time to change Ali's diaper, and then fall asleep holding him. I was tired, no...I was exhausted. I was alone. I was slipping deeper into depression and I didn't know what to do to save myself. I sent Ali's dad a text message saying "You have to help me with him more! I can't do this anymore by myself!" He responded rather quickly. He said "I never told you I wanted a baby." I cried for two days straight. How could he not want this most perfect baby? I never found the answer in him. Instead I found it in myself.

From that day forward I decided I wasn't going to rely on him to make me happy being a mom. It took a while. Years of me waiting for him to step up and help me not struggle with OUR child. Years for me to no longer be surprised when he told me he got arrested, or he couldn't make it, or he didn't have money to help me pay for daycare and other expenses. I stopped relying on him and found my own strength. I began to be grateful for my village. My parents first and foremost, my family, and my closest friends. They all believed in me and filled the void for his inconsistencies. I no longer allow him to get any emotion from me when he doesn't follow through with his word. I found happiness in the little family I had created.

Looking back, I find it super ironic that I cut Ali's umbilical cord. He and I are a team. I released him from my womb and into this world. Our relationship is unmatched. He cares so much about me. Our bond and his compassion and heart make me forget the voids I feel at times being a single parent. I never keep Ali from his father. He sees him about once a week. And I know his dad loves him--- he just doesn't love me. And that is ok. It's actually great, because after five years of being Ali's parent with him I couldn't imagine life with him. But I can't imagine my life without Ali.

Ali saved my life. He is the reason I stopped partying so much. He is the reason I am back in school and running towards my goals. He is the reason I was able to adopt my 13-year-old niece and be a great mom to her as well. He is the reason I smile every day when I wake up and every night before I go to bed. Ali is the reason I have a completely different outlook on life. Happiness isn't found in expectations you have of someone else; happiness is found in yourself. You are in control of the emotions you allow to take over your life. You are in control of the type of person you want to be known as by the universe and all things included. Ali helped me find that happiness in myself. Ali is in love with superheroes, and I am in love with him. My own little superhero in the form of my son. I never wanted kids. But now I couldn't imagine myself being anything or anyone, but the mommy of Ali Alexander and Amaria Lachelle.

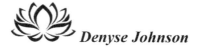 *Denyse Johnson*

Queen's Legacy

In no way, shape, or form, am I under the illusion that anyone really cares about the plight of Black women. Let me be perfectly clear, we are only significant in the context and premise of our own community. No one cares, and frankly they do not want to know. How do I know this? Propaganda is real. Ask any African from the continent of Africa what they are told regarding a relationship with an African American woman. The answer is hands off and stay away from us.

What women will attest to being "lower" on the "totem pole" than an African- American woman? What level of respect does the African American woman have regarding herself, the plight of her husbands and sons? Understanding the lack of resources the African American woman has encourages entities to single us out for abortions, stillborn babies and birth defects. Let me tell you a little of my story as a Black mother...

Divine Natural Essence, born in June of 1997 at 10 am in St. Cloud, MN. Why was she born at this specific time? Because her doctor needed to go on her vacation. It was her vacation time so a C-section ensued regardless of what was best for my baby.

Shakhila Essential Earth born in August of 1999. Upon arriving to the hospital I was told, "Please do not push, she is right there." What was the difference? I stayed home and away from the "medical" doctors and "their" plans, and labored at home because this was my birth and I was attempting to take back the power.
Ijahlee Ann, born at Hennepin County Medical Center in January of 2001. She was breech so she came into the world by C-section like my first-born. The nurse asked me afterwards to rate my pain. I responded with a shrug and told her 5 or 6. She gazed at me for a moment as I adjusted myself in the bed after coming from a walk

around the maternity ward to get some exercise. She then adjusted my meds. The nurse following her shift came in to find me pouring my hot soup down my chest because I was so numb from the opium drip the previous nurse administered. I later found out, the nurse had given me a morphine overdose. When I mentioned to a nurse I was hungry she gave me the left over plate of fruit from another patient.

Ijahman Clinton was born in November of 2002 at St. Paul Regions Hospital where the physician who suctions your throat in surgery decided to take some time away from his post to allow me to suffocate from his neglect. After having Ijahman I noticed his shallow breathing and requested he be looked at. He was taken to the ICU for oxygen and no one came to me and offered to take me to the ICU to be with my sun, so I got up and walked across the hospital enduring the worse pelvic pain I have ever experienced looking for my sun. My breast milk flowed excessively to the point that I left the hospital with 21 bottles of milk. Even with excessive milk the nurses took it upon themselves to still feed Ijahman formula against my wishes. This the ultimate disrespect.

Kalahari W. was stillborn in June of 2009; afterward an intake specialist at Northpoint asked some interesting questions regarding who would be eager for the arrival of Kalahari. I was given an appointment for an ultrasound that was performed with a wand. I had never seen this procedure before. After the conductor of this ultrasound twirled the wand very quickly several time in my uterus, Kalahari was born a few weeks later with his cord wrapped around his neck. I was asked by North Memorial if I wanted an investigation into his death and I responded, "No." They came back with the results of the investigation anyway. The nurse brought Kalahari to me to show me with greater detail the cord wrapped around his neck. What a devil?

Lea-Love Ann born at H.C.M.C the day before a massive snowstorm in December of 2010 and I was verbally attacked by a nurse for objecting to procedures I deemed unnecessary for my child. However, she insisted I was wrong.

Jahseall W. was born in Washington County where my bathroom had a broken toilet and my recovery room had a broken shower. To make a long story short, I have had my fair share of experiences with a system very clear about the worth of a Black woman. Society has given as many obstacles possible to make it difficult and challenging for these children, my children, to be here. As a melanated species we have a natural predator and are hated before we are even born based on that fact alone. There is no way, after all the hell it took to bring these children to this realm I would give them ANYTHING other than breast milk because that was what I could control. Breastmilk was the only thing during this whole process of life and death that I was completely sure of. Completely sure of, without a doubt. The one thing and the one power that could not be taken from me as an African-American woman is my breast milk. We sign away our children to the government each time we sign these birth certificates. Through my breast milk I can relay ancient messages from our past that has traveled through our DNA. You can't take this from me......and still I rise. We have rejected your formula and vaccinations because these children belong to me and I will continue to fight for them.

I have a child in college studying business and economics, another performing in #1 theatre shows, and one taking pre-calculus to take trigonometry before college. We will continue to rise despite the conspiracy to destroy the Black wombman. They are all successful and I did that through all of these experiences.

We must re-establish our brand of motherhood and take our children back completely. When we were in charge of raising this nation's youth we were a force to be reckoned with globally. Now that the United States government is parenting our children we are the laughing stock of the globe. We must build up our families, take back our food, our communities and the world one breastfed baby at a time! We must reconnect with nature, and take the machine out of our existence because it disconnects us from the universe which our life source. I know no one cares about us, and we are at the bottom of the list but you better believe and know we are the only answer to true change. Keep playing if you want. We are the answer. Breastfeed and provide the most optimal start for your seeds. Continue the legacy of raising royalty Black women because if we don't do it, who will?

 **Queen**

Overpouring

I am the product of an absent father and a single mother. Yet, I became a single parent of two daughters by the time I was twenty-two. I experienced abuse as a young girl. And, what others had done to me...in many ways I had done to myself. As a result of that abuse, the *love* I sought had been mostly unhealthy. In a sense, the healing I so desperately needed didn't come until after I became a parent.

I wanted to protect my children from all of that. I wanted their purity to push them to places of passion and joy. I had a job to do and that would require me to protect my daughters from any and every one. I wanted my children to have the world. I wanted them to have all the things I never had. I didn't want them to hurt, experience heartache, or pain. I wanted to be the bearer of it all. So, I *overpoured.*

You see, I grew up in a house with six other children, we had three daddies. The last three children shared a dad, and of the older four, two of them shared a father, but my brother and I had our own daddies. Thing is, they all had relationships with their fathers. Everyone except me. I had my own daddy, but he was married when I was conceived. Didn't help mama at all, it was as if I didn't even exist. He rode down the main highway where I lived daily for over thirty years to get to a job he retired from. He never gave my mother a dime; not for pampers, not for clothes not for food, nothing. I didn't realize how much that affected me until many years later.

So, when I had kids I said they would never want for anything, I wouldn't beg their father for anything, and they would have it all. At least as much as I could give them. I gave birth to two beautiful daughters who turned out to be incredible human beings. I learned how to make it in this world, just for them. I grew up fast when I had my first child, but I became a woman when I gave birth to the second one. I learned how to endure things, and people because I knew I had to take care of my children regardless of what anyone else said or what anyone else was doing.

I dated for a while until I met a good guy, he was everything I would have wanted in a father. Not perfect, but he was darn near close. In fact, he reminded me of the father I only dreamed of. He was handsome, fourteen years older, responsible, distinguished, and loved God. I chose him. In the beginning I didn't trust him to parent my children because they were *mine*. I didn't give him the freedom he needed to be a parent, so he refused to parent. He did all the things a real man does, like made sure we were financially stable, picked them up from school when I couldn't, protected them. When my daughter's manager at McDonald's yelled at her, my husband went to her job and scared the hell out of that man, he has always been our protector. But, he loved my children from a distance, because they were MY children and he *knew* it. If he ever yelled at them, we were all mad at him for days and sometimes weeks. Some things we should have worked out on the front end just never happened in the beginning. I strongly recommend blended families get counseling. My husband was having to live without his own children, yet living with mine day after day. We didn't realize how much that affected him.

We were a blended family, but my children were MY children, I overpoured. I gave my children just about everything they wanted, even if I had to hide it from my husband. We weren't just mother and daughters we were best friends. I saw myself in them and wished I could have had all they had when I was their age. I subconsciously filled an inner void of my own by overextending and *overpouring*. I'm now aware of that and I'm grateful it wasn't to their detriment.

I know I overpoured at times, but I know when it's all said and done my children will be amazing people who will make their mark on this world despite my shortcomings. In some ways, I have my absent father to thank for that. His absence taught me how to be a resilient parent, how to hurt and keep moving, how to fall and get back up, how to lose a love you never really had, but most of all.... he taught me how to love until it hurts.

 **De'Vonna Pittman**

For Baby Girl: It Won't Change, But You Will

I almost didn't write this piece. I began and walked away. Not only because I've had some life challenges thrown at me this year, but because that is what I am accustomed to doing when confronted with "tough stuff." I learned to shut down and restart. I want to thank this certain amazing queen for pushing me to do this; to reflect and lean into the tough stuff to continue to heal.

I don't know what I would do without my mother. She is a good woman with best intentions for the most part. This woman has cared for me and been there for me financially for as long as I can remember. Anything I wanted my mother made it happen for me. She would go without so I would have, a trait that I inherited in my mothering journey as well. My mother would kill for me, she's crazy and yes she has said that. I know she loves and adores me as I her but I know that there is something inside of her that hates me and has made me hate that part of her.

You trust her?

I went to a friend's wedding in my early twenties. I didn't really know too many people but being the social butterfly I am, I mixed and mingled with the other people that were there. I met another girl close to my age which made me excited. Finally someone I can click with! My friend didn't have a lot of girlfriends, so there were mostly older women from the mosque she attended. Through conversation this girl and I started talking about "moms," complaining about them and sharing stories about how crazy and strict they were. And then she added something that had me hell-bent confused: "Through it all though, I can tell my mother *anything*! I go to her first before any of my friends..." She went on to tell me stories about how her mother has given her advice and that she could even talk to her about SEX and her relationship! What?! This was foreign to me, you can **talk** to your mother? I realized, I was 24 years old and would never even think about discussing my personal business with my mother, I always go to friends first! Now I am 30 and I still feel the same.

Now, I am fully aware that there are certain boundaries of conversations in the mother/daughter relationship. I don't want to reveal any graphic details or crazy nights in college to my mother. But as a daughter, if I needed to have a talk like that why can't I go to my mom? But let's forget graphic details or crazy nights in college. Things many daughters should just be able to tell their mothers easily are things I have to contemplate and weigh before beginning to divulge those things to my mother. For example, I refuse to tell her of my son's diagnosis. How? Why? She should know right? Well, yes and no. She is his grandmother, but she's my mother and honestly, I don't trust her with anything I'm not strong enough to handle. And this is something I'm still learning how to handle. I would describe our relationship as "genuinely insincere." I love my mother, I know she loves me. I show her that I care for her and she reciprocates. In this part it is sincere. When it comes to compassion, trust and understanding, it is disingenuous.

Beginning in my early teen years I learned to not tell her things and to consult my peers instead. I remember telling my mother something in our mother-daughter talks, which I used to adore, and the next day, out of anger she used it against me. Out of nowhere, she said…"Well that's why, so and so (repeating what I'd told her the previous day)!" OUCH! I still feel the sting of betrayal from that memory. More recently I consulted her for parenting advice and explained to her how my son was having tantrums and hitting and kicking in his sleep. Of course, this would not stay just between us, because later when we were having a kid discussion with other family members she bolts: "Well that's why your son is fighting you at night. He's so bad!" *Ahhh I remember there was a reason why I don't tell you things!* I mean sometimes I feel like I can be comfortable with her, but she always reminds me not to get too comfortable.

Some have asked me, "Have you ever tried talking to your mom about this?" Oh yes! I used to be called fat ass in my tweens because it was a term of endearment at home. You know things like, "get your fat ass over here and wash these dishes" or "get your fat ass off the couch." This really hurt my feelings, I was sad and insecure as a result of this verbal abuse. The conversation went like this...

"Mom, when you call me fat..."

"Oh Vanessa*, shut up and get out my face!"

I returned to my room and started hitting myself out of anger, frustration and hurt. You can't confront my mother about anything. Her words, actions, and understanding of a given issue and even her wrongs are always right, regardless of how it made you feel. I believe she said: "I am your mother, I can talk to you any way that I feel like." She sees no fault in her flaws. You learn people and what to expect from them. I learned what things I could go to mom with and what I couldn't. It was these failed moments of me having to engage her empathy and kindness that caused me to form the distrust that I have towards her. The distrust of her also makes me question her motives behind her every action. Is this kindness for real? Is this going to be used against me in an argument? Is this to prove some point I may have missed that she was trying to make, or is she just being nice because she can and truly wants to?

I'm mad at him not you!

I feel for those teen girls who are being shamed on YouTube by their mothers for poor choices. Physical harm and demeaning name-calling is not discipline, it's exposing and embarrassing. Why would you want your daughter to feel so low? I cringe at those videos because if social media had been around like this when I was a teen, I wouldn't be surprised if my mother resulted to these tactics to embarrass me. I get angry because I feel that my mother gets a great deal of satisfaction from telling her family and sister-friends about my flaws and failures. I'm almost certain she enjoys it almost as much as she does bragging about my accomplishments.

I am a daddy's girl! I have a great dad but far from perfect as well. My mother knew this. She knew I was a daddy's girl and she took pride in ratting me out to my father. It was like, "Yeah Malcolm, look at Daddy's little princess now!" I remember when I was a young teen and we went on a youth choir trip to an arcade complex. I was hanging out with a friend who was a boy and we had a ball running around playing games and talking. There was some crush element there, I liked him but we were just having fun. My mother felt like I was avoiding her and "sneaking around" behind some boy. When we got home, that was exactly what she told my dad and he beat my ass. Yes, he got the belt and whooped me like I got caught having sex at this place. While I was in shock that he beat me, I was pissed with my mother (though I could not say this to her). She knew very well there was nothing going on, but it gave her a chance to show my father that "she's not so perfect". Another "see, I told you so" for my mother against my dad. It wasn't until I was an adult that she told me she regretted telling him. She said she didn't know he was going to beat me like that...

My mom and dad's relationship issues would also have a direct impact on me. She would also do mean things to me in order to seek revenge on my dad, because it seemed to her, this was a game to be played, and she had to win. Even if that meant hurting his little girl, she would win. One day I was nervously getting ready to leave for my first solo trip out of the country. My first time going abroad on a very long plane ride to a place, I nor anyone in my family had ever been. My family is getting ready to take me to the airport, I'm rushing around for the little "last minute" this and thats. They were mad at each other for something or other, but the excitement wasn't a bit diminished, because it would be okay when I said my goodbyes and got on the plane. We were walking out the door when she announced she wasn't coming. Now? Out of all the times to get mad and decide to play petty, NOW? I broke down and cried. This could be the last time you see me at all should anything happen to this plane, I thought. This is a HUGE step for me. I'm venturing into new worlds, new things and you're not coming to at least see me off? This is the spirit she put in me. A spirit of exploration. A spirit of finding something new and feeding my mind to new opportunities and experiences. I begged her to reconsider and she said, "I know by hurting you it'll hurt him!"

I'm a *hoe*

I was always accused of "sneaking around" or "fucking" when I was in my late teens/early twenties. She flipped out when she found a pair of thongs in the wash and cut them all up. Those were for hoes! I wasn't that type of girl at all. We had went on a gospel choir trip (which she was present for) out of town. The hotel where we stayed had two restaurants literally right next to it, a McDonalds and a KFC. I quite naturally wanted to go to where all my friends were going so I asked my mom for the other key so I could meet her back in the room when we got back. She scoffed, "I'm not giving you no key so you can have sex with a boy while we're gone!" I don't know what I did or what about myself and my mannerisms gave her the impression I was dying to have sex and be this hoe she envisioned me as. This was a gospel youth choir tour! Either way, this projection from her made me too nervous and scared to experiment sexually with anyone anyway out of fear she would find out.

As I got older and started having relationships it changed from "hoe talks" to talks of sadness. Since I've proven that I won't be a hoe, I assumed she would say "great job on not getting pregnant" or "Well, you proved me wrong when I thought you were just out chasing dick." Nope. Instead of being told I'm on the hunt to becoming some sad statistic, I'm getting told that my heartbreak and loneliness is inevitable. "Watch! You will end up in the same kind of fucked up relationship I'm in!" or "Oh and when he cheats on you, you'll be coming back home."

I just wonder why you didn't claim anything positive or speak life into me? How come you didn't say you deserve a better marriage than mine? I wonder if she truly does NOT want me to have a better marriage because hers failed. I know she's a proud woman, but damn, I'm her daughter. I thought the point was to try to make sure the hardships you had are not repeated with me. But it seems as if she wants them to happen so 1- she'll be right, and 2- we can then sit down like mother and daughter and have a miserable conversation about how miserable men are and how they made us miserable.

Impact

Memories and stories can be forgotten or repressed, but the emotional hurt and pain are everlasting. I don't know what I possibly did to deserve this treatment. I love this woman! I love her. I would and still do almost anything to please her. But the distrust, shaming and hurtful words has me at a point where I would never be completely open and honest with her...sometimes I feel fake. I am uncomfortably okay with knowing we may never reach that point because of her stubbornness and inability to change. And no, I am not looking for mom as a best-friend, but I did want to consider my mom a friend. She is not one that I go to for advice in matters of relationships, parenting, or anything that's at the heart of me. When I had my son, she said the same way that you love him, I love you. I want to believe that. I do. But I don't believe it.

I've been working on my relationship with my son since he was inside me. I would talk to him and write to him. I breastfed him for almost 2 ½ years (which my mom ridiculed), not only for the health benefits, but also for our bond. I ended up co-sleeping not only to get sleep but for the closeness to him. I know the Black community would probably say I parent "white," but I don't give a damn. Yes I give my almost 3-year-old choices, and I ask him tons of questions. I want him to know now his opinion matters to me. I seek out help from doctors, therapists and moms to make sure I am doing what is right. I don't know everything, nor do I pretend to. Despite these frustrating, horrible, and sometimes what seem like unbearable "terrible twos," I love this boy unconditionally and open heartedly. I had no choice, but to accept that how he interprets the world is going to be very different from how I did. If my son were to write this 30 years from now I would want him to describe me as loving, uplifting and trustworthy. I want to be everything to him that my mother wasn't to me. I want him to feel he can talk to mom about any and everything, even before he talks to his friends.

I don't know what creates this divide between Black mothers and their daughters. But we need to acknowledge this as a severe problem and do something when we see it happening. Stop posting daughter shaming videos on Facebook and World-Star and confront your friends. This is a cycle we can't repeat again and again. It shouldn't be a rite of passage as a mother to demean your children. We must stop praising Black mothers who subject their girls to this type of treatment and call it good parenting. It is an abuse of authority and exercise of control. Mothers need to educate and empower their daughters on sexuality so they can explore it in the right way. Not shaming a virgin and making her sexually insecure or even acting on your words by calling her a hoe! I'm sure if we delve deeper, we would find similar pain my mother carries from her mother and grandmother. It is not all her fault. Growing up, when I would wish for anything, she would tell me, "Wish in one hand and shit in the other, and see which one gets filled the quickest." She was merely repeating what her mother said to her. Two big takeaways from my mother's parenting is, 1- I can't take my stress and anger of my relationship on him 2-I have to care to listen and listen with no judgement. This is my struggle. I don't want to be my mother to my son, which is hard. I don't want to have a relationship where he doesn't have confidence that I would be there and support him. Some mannerisms are obviously inherited and come natural to me. I hate it, and I'm even embarrassed to admit it, but there were a few times when my mother has come out in my own behavior. I'm battling the part of my mother that's inside me and wants to be hurtful toward my son. But I'm winning! I am blessed and grateful to have a man that knows me, my mother and my story. He is supporting me in this healing, so I can be the best mother to our son, and not anything like her.

 *Vanessa Rose King*

Untitled

I am a wife and mother of six beautiful living children. I have one daughter and six sons. There was a time I didn't think that I was able to conceive any children after my first son. There is a nine-year difference between my first and second born children. Many women probably share my story, especially Black women in North America.

As a young girl, I knew I wanted to be a mother one day. I would have a husband (either Michael Jordan or "The Purple One" Prince) and live in a big mansion. In junior high school I was still playing with dolls, while some of my friends were actually having sex. I wondered what sex would be like. My best friend who was extremely sexually active told me everything I wanted to know. My mother raised four children alone, with no husband and very little support. We were very active in the church and that was the one thing that kept me from giving up my panties at an early age. I was a devout Christian, and proud that I didn't allow temptations to overcome me – my nickname in high school was "Christian Crip." Although I wasn't engaging in any sexual activity, I was surrounded by young ladies who were, and I took on a supportive role for the mothers emotionally and became their doula by default. Most of the girls I helped were in a program that supported young mothers. The **M.I.C.E (Mother's with Infant Children Education)** program was a program for young ladies at South High School who were pregnant and/or had children already. Soon, my best friend at the time was looking for support for her unborn child and herself because she was only 15, pregnant and her parents were very upset about her pregnancy. She actually hid her pregnancy until she was 7 months. She ended up giving her daughter up for adoption and my sister and I played a very vital role for that whole adoption process. My sister and I worked with her and another family to make up adoption arrangements.

Looking at some of the young moms, I didn't have a clue what parenthood was like. From my perspective though, parenthood looked like it was fun and you would always have someone to love you back. I didn't have a real expectation for what it meant to be a parent. I spent many of my teenage years attempting to advocate for many teens moms, but as I think about it in retrospect, I didn't have the experience of being a mom and I probably didn't give them the best advice because of that. Fast forward several years later, at the age of 25, I was married and became a mom to a beautiful son, Jihad. It was at this time I realized how difficult parenting was. My life was no longer "my life," it was "ours." My beautiful **sun**, he was so innocent, and I couldn't see how the world could not love him the way I did. I knew when I gave him the name Jihad, he would have challenges in his life and **he would have to set his own rules, and make his own course in life.**

I would remind him often the meaning and true significance of his name. Jihad Islam Akbar Bey means to fight for what is righteous, because he is great. His name represents the character his father and I wanted to instill in him. Jihad was ready for more siblings and I met someone, and found out I was pregnant at age 31. I was recently divorced, and thought I could share my life with him. He was great with my son as well. After dating for several months I learned I was pregnant. This was a shock to the both of us, we weren't ready for children financially, but I decided to not terminate my pregnancy. I wasn't excited at all about the baby because I didn't feel like I could financially be responsible for another child, especially as a single mother because the child's father didn't want me to keep the baby.

At the time I was working part time and living with a family member. I had no medical insurance coverage. I couldn't even get any prenatal care. I was very concerned about the baby, and I was having issues very early in the pregnancy; I was bleeding and cramping which landed me in the emergency room. I left the hospital feeling hopeless about what was happening to my unborn child and me. I was frustrated with the medical system and felt unsupported in every way imaginable. I did the only thing I knew to do, run.

A few weeks later I decided to pack my bags and move with a good friend that was living in North Carolina. I was able to find the stability and support I needed to raise my family. I was told to apply for medical insurance through the State until my employment medical insurance kicked in. At this point I was already five months pregnant and had not had any prenatal care!

I had an inclination something wasn't right with my unborn child. I couldn't sleep that night. Something felt very wrong in my spirit. I headed to Duke University Emergency Room. After hours of waiting to be seen the doctor finally came in to examine me. He was dead silent as he listened to my belly. He began to walk out of the room before I asked him to tell me what was going on. He told me that everything was fine, he just wanted to give me an ultrasound to check on the baby. About an hour later the ultrasound tech came into the room and began to perform the ultrasound technique I had with my first child. This one seemed so different. She turned the screen away so I wouldn't be able to see the screen. My heart began to race because I knew something was very wrong. All of my questions to her were followed with, "the doctor will explain it." I was preparing myself for a not so good outcome. I began to panic knowing I had a dead baby in me.

Questions ran through my mind. "What did I do wrong? When did this happen? What in the heck is going on?!!!!"

An hour later, yes, an hour, the doctor came in to explain that the baby wasn't alive and they would have to induce my labor. That was the last thing I wanted to do, have a dead baby vaginally. I was put in a wheel chair and taken up to labor and delivery. I called my sister and my best friend to let them know what had happened. They were both with me hours later when the induction began. I labored like most women without the extreme labor pains. Several hours after the induction, I was ready to push out the small baby. The doctor put the baby on my belly and I lost it. I yelled at her to get it off of me, she held it so I could see. This is something I wasn't mentally prepared for. There was no one there to explain what I was feeling, sad, angry and full of questions, and self-doubt.

After two days in the labor unit I was ready to go home, but not before the Chaplin came in to see me. I felt no relief from her visit, only more grief. I was wheeled into the elevator with two moms and their beautiful newborn babies accompanying them. I cried the WHOLE way down to the first floor lobby. I left with no baby and no answers.

At the time, I didn't understand what was going on. I had lost a child and I went through a lot of stress and depression but looking back on the situation I now realized I had turned my own pain into my purpose, and I wanted to work with other women.

Three years later, I met a wonderful man who became my second husband, Malik who would seed me five more healthy children! Our home became a place where there were children everywhere! I enjoyed the laughter, the running around the house, sharing chores, playing games, the arguments; there was never a dull moment at our place. I am a mother to six children, but I feel like I have the privilege and opportunity to mother my clients as a doula and birth worker. I am not the mother that has the opportunity to stay at home with my children during the day. I am responsible for securing Black and Brown, low-income mom's birth support, postpartum and mental health support from providers that are culturally appropriate because I understand the importance of having someone who shares your background to help you through the most trying times of your life as a wombman and mother. My job is to make sure mothers and their families feel safe, respected and empowered to have the birth they desire. I wasn't prepared enough to have my last five children vaginally. I did not know I could have had a VBAC because I was not educated about my options.

I started Ahavah Birth Works in 2015 because I saw a need for women to have support through their pregnancy and birthing experience. I know the importance of having someone that can culturally relate to a wombman and most of all celebrate her and her unborn child. We go through pregnancies as if we need to have an excuse for getting pregnant. Our babies from the womb aren't being celebrated. Ahavah was built with the intentions of celebrating and supporting the wombmen in our community. Black lives matter, starting from the womb. I hope my story will encourage women to seek out a doula that can help navigate them through a sometimes rough medical world as well as be there for you to support your emotional and educational needs throughout the pregnancy.

I am learning that being a mother requires us to provide the same principles of compassion, love, unity, understanding, and closeness with nature not only to our own biological children, but to our husbands, boo thangs, sisters, uncles, aunts, the nation, world, and planet. We are the mothers, the cornerstones and the pillars of the community, and we are rebuilding beginning from the womb of our minds, which ultimately is intricately connected to our physical womb.

 *Clara Sharp*

Suffering in Silence... #RealTalk

Peace & Greetings All,

Wellness wished to all who read this. This is an open letter to all the ladies out there. Never mind me though, I'm just a girl from the Midwest who is the eldest child born to a large family. As I'm sitting here writing this letter, it's one I have been thinking about over time since being asked to write a piece and share my story. I'm sitting here on the floor thinking of all I want to say, so it looks like I'm going to have to pour out freely from my heart. As I thought about doing this, I thought about where I am NOW and it's because of where I've been in the past. I'm at a place in life right now where I'm ready to "move on" (inside joke). I'm realizing how much I have been focusing on the past and how much I'm allowing it to keep me from being who I AM, and I'm no longer interested in *how* I am. Those are two different things. I'm done with how I am! Who I AM is much more liberating. I'm at a place in life where I have chosen to "let it go," (lol, I'll probably be using lots of those) ☺...

I digress... I was asked to write this piece, and when initially asked, I was wondering what to share. I thought and thought and thought AND thought about that since I had recently realized how I had been suffering in silence with most of the instances in my life that (silence) would be my focus. I soon afterwards saw the beautiful young lady who sent out the request post stating the focus of the pieces were around suffering in silence... AMAZING!!! And right on time for me, as I am a person who loves synchronicity.

I guess I would have to start in chronological order because that's just how I roll. As a person who lives with anxiety, it's how I have control over what and how I remember. It's not really so much one specific time as much as it is "A" time. This is about the time when my parents chose to let me go, I mean really let me go, and on top of that, they let me go with them... (sigh)... my grandparents... my dad's parents. These people were already creeping into middle age when they had my dad. They were in their 50's and 60's when I was born around the end of the 70's decade. My mom says I asked to live with them, BUT I don't know who in the hell lets a three to four year old kid make life altering decisions like that, but that's none of myyyy... oh wait, maybe it is my business because that's where my suffering truly began, I believe.

So she says I asked, huh? Because now I'm way more reflective and thinking about what makes sense. See around this time, I was born, of course, and my sister of the same parents was born a little less than a year after me. Where it gets tricky, though, is that another little sister follows her just four months later than that... yeah, you know what that means... DRAMA!!! And we know relationship drama is the worst drama ever. They were married and ole girl (the side chick) was young as hell... (singing that church song Further along you'll know all about it, further along you'll understand why). In retrospect, I see why I may have asked to go with some old folks who were 50-60 some odd years my senior. Y'all know they ain't have NO relationship nothing going on, well, you know the average BS that comes with being together. I musta found solace there, but did not realize the suffering that was on the other side of the solace.

There are extremes, right, so they're going to accompany one another on this journey. I went there, but after I did, it made me realize how much of a different world I put myself in. I was constantly being asked by my peers if my parents were dead or lived out of town and stuff. I'd be longing for interactions with my parents, and usually they were to no avail. I got tired of going to church with Granny and Granddaddy, yet, it was about the only social life I had.

Oh yeah, there was the time I burned myself because I was playing with a lighter left behind by a supposed to be responsible adult. I was rushed to the hospital to be there for nearly a month with second degree burns and barely saw their faces, but you know who was there EVERYDAY. Imagine being the "other" daughter introduced to your mom's friends and being a child of a dude who continued to have many lady friends, crossing your fingers as you call a parent wishing for them to be home and available to talk to you, but you start to get the picture. And, on top of this no one cared. No one asked if I was okay, if I needed anything or if there was anything they could do. There's no hand reaching out or a listening ear... so, I fell back and gathered that I must not really matter. So, I suffered in silence... (Singing, "Nobody Not Really" by Alicia Keys)...

Which brings me to being about seven years old. I had two older cousins who were regular visitors on the weekend.

They were like six to seven years older than me. They were like big brothers to me. Well, one day, I got caught sneaking candy (hmmmm...) and in order for them to not tell on me, I had to agree to some other sneaky behavior. You know what I mean ;-) This was the older one's idea. Awww, excuse him, he's a product of incest. Anywho, this took some years and for the sake of time, let's just skip to the part where I NEVER told anyone, well except for my future boo, you know, the one of my dreams (?), but otherwise, you know me--- I suffered in silence...

(Singing On to the next, on, on, to the next one (in my Jay Z and Swizz Beats voice). Now, I don't even really think about all that stuff I used to be challenged with. I had some boyfriends as I started growing up and thangs. Gave my stuff to some dudes who didn't deserve this top grade **(not as many as some of my friends, but enough)**. Till I met my boo! Yeah, him was different. Not different from me, we had a lot in common, you know like Bobby and Whitney. He was different from the other dudes I had given my stuff to. He really cared about me and we were friends first. We use to kick it! You know how it's all peaches and cream in the beginning? And, boy there was a lot of cream, lol... Whew... O...K... Things were going pretty good at first, and about a year into the relationship, I got pregnant. I "was only 17 in this mad man's dream **(in my Slick Rick voice)**" and was entering my senior year of high school. This is when the boat started rocking. Things were definitely changing.

My baby was due in February of the following year and around about December, I started hearing these rumors about some other chick. I dismissed them, though, because that didn't sound like him. He was different, right? Nah, he wasn't, really. After the baby was born, I found out that the swirling rumors had some truth, and THAT BITCH, oops, I mean, the chick was not someone I thought to be his taste, but nonetheless, it was happening. To make a VERY long story short, I got tangled up in a love triangle that lasted nearly five years with us (me & "the chick") taking turns having babies for this (derogatory racial slur beginning with an "N"). Then, to add insult to injury, I repeated a pattern I swore I wouldn't be a part of AS me and ole girl had kids just four months a part of one another. I had almost become a carbon copy of my mother's situation at this point, minus the giving away of kids. I tell you another pattern fulfilled at this point, too. I mean the obvious cannot be avoided, as all who knew and witnessed the pregnancies and the babies of "the other woman," but what few got to see, directly, was my pain, agony, and what seemed like defeat. You know why? If you don't know me by now, you will never, never, never know me **(sing it in your head...)** because if you've been paying attention, you'd know beyond a shadow of a doubt, that *I... SUFFERED... IN... SILENCE...* (chorus of Window Seat by Erykah Badu playing in the background).

This is Midwest Girl. Midwest girl was silly. Don't be like this Midwest girl, EXPRESS YOURSELF.

Mourning

I'm mourning
I'm mourning all the things I was told I couldn't
All the things I did not have time to mourn
I'm mourning all the things I wanted that failed
All the things I needed and didn't get...

I'm tired of being told that I must move on
That I must push through
That my sadness makes me weak
That I'm wrong for feeling this way
And that I shouldn't be so meek...

Watch me mourn for all I've lost
And for all things lost by my mothers before me
Praise me for how well I weep
How deep my pool of tears flows
After mourning comes understanding
Then imagine how dangerous I'll be...

 *Amber Alexis*

S'sence

Live in S'sence... Not me, but you...
Now the joy of my world lives in you...

You changed me, you loved me, you made me who I am
You changed me, you loved me, you made me who I am
You changed me, you loved me, you made me who I am
You changed me, you loved me, you made me who I am

So at this time in my life, I was going through an identity crisis. So I think I had like half of my hair long and a fade on the other side and it was a true reflection of the way I was feeling about myself. I was just in a tug of war and then I remember my back starting to hurt and I was having these lower abdominal pains and boobs just started to get really unfun. I remember going to the hospital and thinking that clearly I got the flu! Something was wrong with me on the inside and I couldn't explain it. Something was changing on the inside and I couldn't really explain what it was but all of it was too much. I remember sitting in the room, and y'all I have narcolepsy so fall asleep at the drop of a dime if I'm not talking or engaged, so I remember falling asleep in the bed and waking up in the ultrasound room and I was like ummmmmm, excuse me. And I remember the nurse telling me "we're going to see how far along you are", and I remember telling her "wrong girl, I came here because I had abdominal pains, my back was hurting and my breasts aren't feeling so hot." She said, "Yeah, um, you're pregnant!" The way that I cried instantly, all on the floor and everything, I'm so serious. The nurse asked me, "Well, how many children do you already have?" I said, "NONE!" She gave me that "girlllllllll, look", like you are crying like you got 6 already. I just remember feeling, "Not me! Not me! Not me!" because where I come from having a baby is like a curse. Having a baby means you failed. Having a baby when you have not been considered

successful by someone else's definition means that you are unsuccessful.
But you.... *points to her daughter, Baby S'sence, in the crowd...*
You changed me
As you began to grow inside of mommy's belly you helped with my definition
More importantly, from the inside out, you loved me!
Even after you get a whopping you still love me.
Even when I tell you no, you still say "mommy, I love you!"

This Black, pretty girl, not feeling enough...
Feeling unworthy to be loved...
Feeling unworthy to know love...
Feeling unworthy to be called "momma, mommy, mother."
But you, you changed me.
I was going on a downhill spiral...

You changed me, you loved me, you made me who I am
You changed me, you loved me, you made me who I am
You changed me, you loved me, you made me who I am
You changed me, you loved me, you made me who I am

In a world where I felt like I had to impress people
This infant, this child, this toddler, she changed me, she loved me
I was able to see how God really worked then...
You made me who I am.
You changed me, you loved me, you made me who I am
You changed me, you loved me, you made me who I am
You changed me, you loved me, you made me who I am
You changed me, you loved me, you made me who I am

Now the joy, now the joy, now the joy of my world lives in S'sence
Now the joy of my world lives in S'sence
Now the joy of my world lives in S'sence
Now the joy of my world lives in S'sence

You changed me, you loved me, you made me who I am
You changed me, you loved me, you made me who I am
You changed me, you loved me, you made me who I am
You changed me, you loved me, you made me who I am

That's all that I desire that you know baby...
I remember praying to God for a husband.
I remember praying to Him asking for genuine friends.
I remember asking for a closer relationship with my family but
baby He gave me you.
He knew that you were enough for me.

And every time I was feeling like I wasn't it, you would say,
"momma, I love you."
It was like your words began to drown my insecurities.
Your love began to choke out those unsure feelings.
So as I was on a journey feeling like I was alone
He knew that you would change the dynamics in me.
There was something about you, your smile, your laugh, your
sassy walk, your sassy talk.

I even remember when I was younger wishing that I was light
skinned.
Wishing that my hair looked a certain way.
Somehow I thought that I would be more beautiful.
And so when you came out of me, I just pictured God laughing
loudly and saying "no matter how I create you, you're
beautiful."
Because baby, you look like your momma.
So in the times where people said, "a child meant that you
were going to be unsuccessful", you helped clear that
definition. I realized one of my greatest accomplishments is
you and everyday you give me an opportunity to prove that.

You changed me, you loved me, you made me who I am
You changed me, you loved me, you made me who I am

You changed me, you loved me, you made me who I am
You changed me, you loved me, you made me who I am

S'Sence Adams, Spoken Word Artist and Creator
of Herstory and Love Unleashed

Verbal Bouquet (Happy Mother's Day)

An expression of love and appreciation through the written words of a grown Black man and dedication to his single mother of five.

(Happy Mother's Day to all of the mothers out there. Happy Mother's Day to my mother in particular. I guess because you can call it a verbal bouquet since I'm not there. You're the most caring and wonderful, intelligent, witty, resourceful, relentless, nurturing mom that I could ever imagine or that I could ever hope for).

I don't talk to you like I should, I barely pick up the phone
Phony excuses only remind me I ain't grown
Growing pains felt, gotta make it on my own
Tryna be the man in a land away from home
For now I'm all alone, living on what you taught me
Little bitty doses of the bitter Black coffee
Gave it to me no filter, the alternative was costly
You knew if you didn't wake me, they would put me in a coffin
You fixed coughing with affection, kisses, and blessings
NyQuil, Vick's and rubbed it on my chest then
Tucked me in tight
As I write this, I can see
Why you kept telling me I'll be all I wanna be
Little me in the kitchen tip-toeing to watch
Watching how you cooked in every skillet, every pot
Very hot stove, even used to heat the household
Everybody loves you Mama, you sweet devout soul
You teach me now, oh, ooh-we, I 'bout froze
Truly, a sound goes through me, then outros
Loose leaf - I use to capture what I remember, see...

And light up your face
How you used to do every Christmas tree
Memories bring the tears to me when I think on the struggle
Single mother, five kids, but the cards didn't trump you.
How did you keep rising when the world aint' seem to love you?
Kept a heart up your sleeve, never needed to reshuffle
I believe in, and I love you.
And equally you encourage me
Despite the starvation
We made it and you gave birth to me
For everything you've sacrificed, I'm indebted eternally
Monetarily, physically, here's a deposit, verbally
Literally you're the world to me.
That is not a hyperbole
It has taken each year to see how you did this so purposefully
Resented when you would curse at me, but I knew you meant it
Funny cause you're cursing is what led to me repenting
I'mma gon' ahead and end this proclamation of thanks
My intoxication of love for you just leaves me blank
I struggle just to say thanks for your miracles today
So I figured I'd deliver this lyrical bouquet
Despite the distance, the present's a miracle today
So I wanna deliver this lyrical bouquet
Mama, smell each rose with your ears today
I just hope you can enjoy this lyrical bouquet
I love you, Mama

 A.C Lewis

Woman as Mother: Part II

Woman as Mother pour into life
Modeling peace as an option
Or she can set a standard to swear, smoke and not accept tears
And release pain through violence
If that is what she chooses to do
Then that is what she will teach

Woman as Mother
Must work on the inside
Her children are her last shot and her first gift
She betting on them to be better than her
Her behavior is what they are watching

Woman as Mother
Shows up just in time
Skilled and compartmentalized
She may have birthed a child that many eyes watched grow
Or a child that didn't get much time
The unseen child that lives within her fake smiles
Which unnecessary secrets help hide

When she sees babies and gets that feeling inside
Cherishing unlived memories and images of what the world would have been like

Woman as Mother is always Birthing
Notice the walk of woman as mother
Bags in hand, menu in mind, lessons to share
With a child that will impact their future

Realize her steps like checkers or chess

The mother as woman strides, picking and choosing through systems that want to tell her how to teach, feed, and care for her child

Pray for the young girl as mother, who will have to grow up and raise a child at the same damn time
Offer her your time if she needs a break
Ask her questions with the goal of internal thought
That do not need right answers right away
She models the choices of how to live
Her life is a movie and the audience comes without audition
And they will soon be her supporting cast

Does she disregard the importance of her walk?
It is imperative to the type of life
That the future will write
Her rituals and rhythm, her meals and music,
Her responses and relationships will be reflected in her harvest
Nurture the woman as mother
Sometimes she is thirsting for attention to feed the little girl inside

Pour fresh energy anew into her mind and spirit
Challenge her thoughts, and behaviors about whom she shares her womb with
Without judgment, listen to her same story over and over again, it will help her

Provide to woman as mother a safe space to release
Share with her options that contradict the 4 choices,
1 right answer
Idea or oppression
Encourage her rest

Pour her cups of water
Hold her hands
Let her breathe deep
Let her reflect and be deliberate
Support her when her back won't straighten because it
has been bent so much
Stand with her in her dreams
Point to where you see them in the sky
Remember with her the ancestors
Even babies that she misses so much that she cannot
begin to even explain
Use your hands to wet her a towel for her tears
Allow her to break knowing that you cannot fix her
Her repair is from within after the release of things
beyond her control
Share with her your trials, lessons and successes
She will keep them in her medicine bag
Feed her good live food
Tell her it will be okay
Believe in life with her and walk knowing that you have
made a space for woman as mother to live, birth, and love
Give her silence
Let her decide when to share her voice
Give her paper and pencil
Give her soil and seed
Paint and easel
Needle and thread
She is the mender and the healer of the family
Watch her pace when she returns
Sit in the shine from her smile
Dedicate time to collect her wisdom in baskets
Knowledge for building a foundation
Watch how she navigates the spring water sea
On dry concrete land
The uncharted steps of woman as mother

Thank her for the last bite
That she gives reluctantly and willingly
Embrace her duality
Motherhood, courage good
The holder of life, not too tight or you will crush, especially if you rush it

First teacher
Even without words, vibrations and sensations transmitted through umbilical cord
Let her teach and nurture thinkers with self-respect and courage
Because from her bosom can come scholars with innovations and choices
Or murderers who were once leaders with misplaced energy in

A system-controlled environment
She is
And without her we are not....
And where we are is a result of, where she was led, where she was taken, what she believed
And what she was fed

Speak her life and she will speak them life, and they will live
And begin to speak life as well
A legacy stronger to share
Woman as Mothers, the Creator's assistant
What is she creating now?

 *Princess Titus*

Ubuntu Minneapolis

And

Black Lotus Mothers

In the
fall of 2015, Jasmine Tane't Boudah, and a sister-
mother friend, Nina Roberts sat down and decided to
create a small and intimate community initiative called
Ubuntu Minneapolis as a direct result of the gaps in
service they noticed in the community. Ubuntu
Minneapolis is a community breastfeeding, parenting,
and literacy initiative that aims to inspire parents to be
the first teachers of their children. The goal is to spread

awareness about the many benefits of breastfeeding for both the mother and children, encourage positive parenting and awareness about child brain development and to provide the tools and support to parents.

At its core, Ubuntu Minneapolis is about embodying the philosophy and humanitarianism approach, acknowledging that all of our fates are intricately linked and bound to one another. Seen in this way, we can no longer sit helplessly and watch as our people are taken advantage of and inherently failed and undeserved. The essence of Ubuntu is the concept of "I am because you are." According to Bishop Tutu, "It is the essence of being human. **UBUNTU** speaks of the fact that my humanity is caught up and is inextricably bound up in yours. I am human because I belong. It speaks about wholeness, it speaks about compassion." Seen in this light, the pair operate wholeheartedly with this mindset.

Shortly after beginning the work of Ubuntu, Black Lotus Mothers was birthed to provide educational, emotional, and physical support to any Black mothers encountered by Jasmine, Nina, and other mothers looking to serve their community. Black Lotus Mothers has an online presence with a closed Facebook group where Black mothers can come to share their stories, seek support and even advice about their journey as a Black mother.

In addition to this, the group meets often to provide holistic support to encourage healing and progress toward growth and development while offering a helping hand when needed. Much of the reality of Black mothers is we spend so much time taking care of everyone else and being confronted by the Black superwoman complex that many of us never ask for help. Black Lotus mothers is striving to break through barriers and mother the mothers in true sisterhood so they can pour into their families, children and communities.

Much of the work is done through focus groups and individualized support from either Jasmine or Nina. The goal is to work with women as they mother through pain and help them understand that they do not have to suffer in silence. Black Lotus Mothers operates with the understanding that although we are strong Black women we all need support and a village behind us because mothering was not intended to be done alone. To date Black Lotus Mothers has participants across the nation who receive support while mothering, including many of the contributing authors of this compilation.

Thank you for supporting our work!

Any proceeds from the book Black Lotus **Mothers Mothering Through Pain and Suffering In Silence: A Collection of Stories from Survivors** will go directly to the Ubuntu work in Minneapolis.

If you have any questions or would like to get involved, volunteer or simply learn more about the work we are striving to do in collaboration with other organizations, please feel free to contact us at ubuntuminneapolis@gmail.com, via Instagram at @BlackLotusMother or Twitter @BlackLotusMa.

Made in the USA
Monee, IL
10 June 2021

70909811R00128